Social Investment and Economic Growth

A Strategy to Eradicate Poverty

Patrick Watt

Oxfam

HC
79
P63
W38
2000

front cover photograph: Camp Number One Primary School, Sankore, Ghana (Sarah Errington/Oxfam)

First published by Oxfam GB in 2000

© Oxfam GB 2000

ISBN 0 85598 434 1

A catalogue record for this publication is available from the British Library.

Available from the following agents:

USA: Stylus Publishing LLC, PO Box 605, Herndon, VA 20172-0605, USA
tel: +1 (0)703 661 1581; fax: + 1(0)703 661 1547; email: styluspub@aol.com
Canada: Fernwood Books Ltd, PO Box 9409, Stn. 'A', Halifax, N.S. B3K 5S3, Canada
tel: +1 (0)902 422 3302; fax: +1 (0)902 422 3179; e-mail: fernwood@istar.ca
India: Maya Publishers Pvt Ltd, 113-B, Shapur Jat, New Delhi-110049, India
tel: +91 (0)11 649 4850; fax: +91 (0)11 649 1039; email: surit@del2.vsnl.net.in
K Krishnamurthy, 23 Thanikachalan Road, Madras 600017, India
tel: +91 (0)44 434 4519; fax: +91 (0)44 434 2009; email: ksm@md2.vsnl.net.in
South Africa, Zimbabwe, Botswana, Lesotho, Namibia, Swaziland: David Philip Publishers, PO Box 23408, Claremont 7735, South Africa
tel: +27 (0)21 64 4136; fax: +27(0)21 64 3358; email: dppsales@iafrica.com
Tanzania: Mkuki na Nyota Publishers, PO Box 4246, Dar es Salaam, Tanzania
tel/fax: +255 (0)51 180479, email: mkuki@ud.co.tz
Australia: Bush Books, PO Box 1958, Gosford, NSW 2250, Australia
tel: +61 (0)2 043 233 274; fax: +61 (0)2 092 122 468, email: bushbook@ozemail.com.au
Rest of the world: contact Oxfam Publishing, 274 Banbury Road, Oxford OX2 7DZ, UK.
tel. +44 (0)1865 311311; fax +44 (0)1865 313925; email publish@oxfam.org.uk

Published by Oxfam GB, 274 Banbury Road, Oxford OX2 7DZ, UK

Oxfam GB is a registered charity, no. 202 918, and is a member of Oxfam International.

Contents

Tables

Figures

Boxes

Acknowledgements

Many Oxfam staff have contributed to this book, too numerous to mention by name. Particular thanks should go to Kevin Watkins, who has provided invaluable comments and support. Thanks should also go to Ruth Mayne, who provided substantial input into Chapter 3, and to Dianna Melrose, Fran Bennett, Caroline Sweetman, Sarah Totterdell, and Catherine Robinson. The book has benefited from discussions with all these colleagues. Ruth Pearson of the University of East Anglia and Pamela Lowden of the University of Oxford also gave many helpful comments and criticisms of the first draft of the book, which greatly improved the text.

Patrick Watt

Introduction

Growth with equity

We live in a world of unprecedented prosperity. It is now perfectly practicable to ensure that every person's basic rights — enough food to eat, clean water to drink, access to basic health services, and the opportunity to be educated — are respected. For the first time in human history, the knowledge and the means exist to make the eradication of poverty a realisable goal. Yet one quarter of all people continue to live in poverty, unable to meet even their most basic needs. This failure to convert global prosperity into rapid and substantial poverty reduction ought to be viewed as inexcusable. This book examines some of the ways in which wealth creation can be harnessed to meet the needs of the poor and disempowered, as well as the needs of the wealthy and powerful.

Since Oxfam began its work in 1942, the world has altered radically. The human population has more than tripled, and the urban population has increased rapidly. The socialist bloc of centrally planned economies has ceased to exist, and major new markets have developed. Women have won for themselves a political voice they were previously denied, and democratic systems of government have become the rule, rather than the exception. Perhaps most extraordinary of all, however, has been the improvement in the standard of living experienced by hundreds of millions of people in the last fifty years. These achievements in reducing levels of material deprivation, sickness, and early death are truly remarkable.

Great progress has been made ...

In the past 50 years, poverty has declined more than it did in the past 500 years. With the end of colonialism in most of Africa and Asia, the provision of health care and education, clean water, and adequate nutrition was extended to millions of people. The global economy grew at a rapid pace, even in sub-Saharan Africa and South Asia, and the period from 1950 to the early 1970s was regarded by many as the 'golden age of capitalism'. This economic growth provided people with new livelihood opportunities, and governments with the means to make crucial social investments. Major improvements in living standards were registered. Even in the poorest countries, life expectancy increased by more than ten years. Child mortality has been reduced by more than half. Most children, for the first time in human history, have been given the opportunity to learn to read and write. In most parts of the South, these advances in human welfare continue to be consolidated and extended, albeit at an unacceptably slow pace. Yet despite these advances, the benefits of economic growth have been distributed inequitably, and development has been uneven. Unmet basic needs and extreme material deprivation remain a daily reality for hundreds of millions of people. The need for Oxfam's work, and the work of other agents for change, remains as urgent today as it was half a century ago.

Great challenges remain ...

One quarter of the world's people continue to live in absolute poverty, unable to meet their most basic needs, and surviving on less than a dollar a day, the World Bank's international poverty line. Over one hundred million children of school age are denied the right to a basic education, and in sub-Saharan Africa the absolute and proportionate numbers of children out of school are rising. Girls continue to be actively discriminated against in access to education: two thirds of the children who are not in primary school are female. Each *year*, half a million women die in childbirth because they have no access to simple and affordable ante-natal health care. Every *week*, close to a quarter of a million children under the age of five die from easily preventable diseases.

The slow response on the part of governments and the international organisations to these vast unmet needs is shameful. While the wealthy creditor nations are able within a matter of weeks to mobilise tens of billions of dollars to bail out private investors in East Asia or Latin America, the scandal of poverty is met with indifference. A renewed political commitment to poverty eradication is urgently needed on the part of governments both in the North and in the South.

Two messages and two challenges

This book carries two messages. First, *absolute poverty is not inevitable*. Second, *equitable economic growth is a necessary condition for poverty eradication*. Equitable growth means giving people who live in poverty genuine opportunities to participate in markets and make the key decisions that shape their futures. Equity implies recourse to the core principles of justice. As an organisation committed to economic and social justice, equity is at the core of Oxfam's work.

From these two messages, two challenges can be issued to the international community. First, *to achieve a return to rapid economic growth*. Economic growth is crucial to building on the progress that has been made in poverty reduction to date. Rising wealth not only increases the ability of people to meet their basic needs in markets: it allows the state to tax more, and spend more on infrastructure and services with a high public-goods content. The wealth that has been generated in the industrial countries through sustained and equitable growth has funded dramatic improvements in living standards. These improvements fed back into the growth process: advances in education and health care contributed to productivity increases, and the effective investment of increasing tax revenues created a virtuous circle of further growth and rising living standards.

Conversely, economic stagnation reduces the resources available to the state, while falls in per capita income also make it more difficult for the poor to meet their basic needs in the market, making people more vulnerable to poverty and less productive economically. A return to growth is badly needed in those East Asian, transitional, and Latin American countries worst hit by the financial crisis which began in 1997. Financial instability and falling incomes have reversed many of the development gains of recent years, threatening longer-term recovery prospects. Yet the need for growth is most urgent in sub-Saharan Africa, the world's poorest and most marginalised region. Here, per capita incomes fell still further between 1990 and 1996, and are now at the same level as they were 25 years ago. Many of the development gains of the initial post-independence period have been eroded by economic stagnation and conflict, and the consequent failure of states to meet their citizens' most basic needs. Despite modest economic recovery in sub-Saharan Africa in the second half of the 1990s, the impact on poverty levels has been weak, and the benefits of growth have not been evenly distributed.

The failure to convert growth into rapid poverty reduction points to the second development challenge. This is *to realise the potential developmental gains of rapid economic growth.* Growth is a necessary but not sufficient condition for poverty eradication. The initial distribution of resources in a society has a crucial bearing on the efficiency with which growth reduces poverty levels. The more unequal the society, the higher the growth rate needed to achieve a given rate of poverty reduction. The development strategy pursued is also a key factor. For poverty eradication to happen, growth must be labour-intensive, providing viable livelihood opportunities for poor people. Public investment in good-quality basic social provision must be the foremost priority of governments. And pro-poor development strategies are needed. These objectives have to be pursued simultaneously, and as part of an integrated strategy, for poverty to be eradicated. Treating issues of distribution as separate from economic growth is at best misguided: the form that growth takes is crucial in determining whether or not it actually enhances human welfare.

The core policies for delivering growth with equity

This book identifies core policies to facilitate development for all. It draws on Oxfam's programme experience, and more generally on Oxfam's experience of working with communities who have been excluded from general trends towards prosperity. This experience has informed the recommendations for reforming public policy that are made at the end of each chapter. In the final chapter a distillation of these recommendations is offered.

Three core recommendations are made in this book.

■ Public investment in good-quality basic universal social provision — 'human capital investment' — is crucial to achieving rapid and substantial poverty reduction. Education and health care are basic rights, which enhance individual well-being and strengthen the ability of people to claim other rights. But investing in education and health also raises productivity levels and is a necessary foundation for wealth creation, allowing societies to move into production with higher added value.

■ In an increasingly urbanised and market-oriented world, labour-market status and poverty are ever more closely connected. Governments, through protection of minimum labour standards, investment in education and training, a stable macro-economic environment, investment incentives, and strategic use of foreign investment, can actively promote pro-poor labour-intensive growth.

■ Rural development requires pro-poor policies. In many instances, land redistribution is an important component of rural development strategy. Other core policies to facilitate rural development are investment in physical and communications infrastructure, stable prices for basic foodstuffs, access to credit and savings facilities, good-quality social provision, and access to relevant technologies.

An outline of the themes

In the first chapter of this book, the relationship between growth, poverty, and equity is examined. Poverty eradication is defined, and the role of economic growth in poverty eradication is discussed. The role of distribution in poverty eradication is then examined. The distribution of income, assets, and public spending is a major factor in the distribution of growth. It is argued that inequality is inimical to sustained and rapid growth, and that it carries social, political, and economic costs. Rather than growth being achievable only at the cost of equity (and vice versa), the two are shown to be mutually reinforcing. Equitable societies tend to have faster economic growth and more stable political and social systems than highly unequal societies. The section concludes by arguing that pursuing poverty eradication requires an active development strategy on the part of the state, ensuring that growth is directed to the end of enhancing human welfare.

In the second chapter, the importance of getting the fundamentals of social provision right is considered. The link between social investment and growth is illustrated. The best ways of achieving universal provision of basic social services are then discussed. The problems associated with cost-recovery policies and marketisation of basic social services in poor countries are examined. Ways of extending access to basic services through raising demand and improving supply are discussed in the second half of the chapter.

Promoting sustainable livelihoods as part of a development strategy is the theme of the third chapter. Social investments (discussed in the previous chapter) must generate genuine livelihood opportunities. Labour is the key asset of the poor, and labour-intensive growth strategies are crucial to poverty eradication. The costs of under-utilised labour are briefly considered. The chapter goes on to examine the implications of rapid urbanisation for poverty eradication and livelihood creation, and strategies for promoting development in rural areas, where poverty continues to be concentrated. In the final section of the chapter, the implications of trends towards globalisation are discussed.

The final chapter summarises the policy recommendations made in earlier chapters.

1 Growth, equity, and poverty eradication

Growth, poverty, and equity

Writing two and a half thousand years ago, the Greek philosopher Aristotle observed that wealth 'is evidently not the good we are seeking; for it is merely useful for the sake of something else'.[1] In other words, growth is simply one means to the end of improving human well-being, which is the ultimate purpose of development in its broadest sense. This is a seemingly obvious distinction, but it is one that is prone to be forgotten: growth is an indispensable tool for achieving development, but only if we direct growth to providing the 'something else' that Aristotle wrote about. This book considers the ends to which growth is a means, and how growth might best be directed to meeting those ends.

Poverty eradication makes good economic sense, as well as being a moral imperative. Poverty is not inevitable, and, while the target of eradicating extreme poverty is ambitious, it is far from impossible. The experience of the last 50 years demonstrates this clearly. Sustained and largely equitable economic growth took place both in the industrialised North and in the developing countries of the South between the 1950s and the late 1970s. This laid the foundations for rapid improvements in material wellbeing, and gave hundreds of millions of people a standard of living that would have been astonishing to their grandparents. During the lives of the last two generations, the reduction in levels of material deprivation, sickness, and early death in the developing world is historically unprecedented, and all too often overlooked. There is no good reason why these on-going improvements in living standards should not be consolidated and extended to benefit the millions of people who continue to live in poverty.

In almost every country in the last 50 years, income poverty has been reduced and morbidity and mortality rates have been dramatically lowered. Even in the poorest regions, life expectancy has increased by more than a decade, and child mortality has been halved in the last 50 years. Meanwhile, for the first time in human history, the majority of people are being given the opportunity to learn to read and write. Rising wealth and the growth of the state have been decisive factors in these achievements. Average per capita income in developing countries has increased threefold since 1950, and considerably faster in East Asia, and this has allowed states to tax more, and spend more on infrastructure and services with a high public-goods content.

Much has been done towards meeting the goal of poverty eradication, but huge sections of the world's population continue to be excluded from the benefits of growth. The 550 million people living in the 49 Least Developed Countries (LLDCs) have suffered reversals in living standards in the last decade, and in many countries in sub-Saharan Africa school enrolment, life expectancy, and nutritional intake are at approximately the same levels as 25 years ago. Women and children in particular have often failed to benefit from economic growth; they account for a disproportionate section of the world's poor people. In every society, people's opportunities to participate in growth in ways that enhance their well-being are restricted, because of marginalisation, ill health, a lack of education, and poverty.

In short, despite the progress made in the last 50 years, the scale of unmet human need remains enormous. One third of the population of the developing world continues to live in extreme poverty; more than 100 million children of school age are denied the right to an education; and every day 35,000 children under the age of five die from preventable diseases. The persistence of such extreme poverty, at the close of a century of unparalleled progress, is an indictment of the way in which the post-1945 vision of a globally shared freedom and prosperity has been betrayed.

There is a fundamental obstacle to more rapid poverty eradication and the completion of this unfinished agenda. This barrier is inequality. We live in a world fissured by huge and unprecedented disparities in wealth and opportunity. Moreover, these disparities have been growing ever more rapidly in recent years. In 1960, the wealthiest fifth of the world's population had an average income some thirty times larger than the world's poorest fifth. In 1990 the 'income-share ratio' stood at 60:1. Today it stands at 78:1. Much of this wealth is concentrated in the hands of a tiny group of individuals. The richest ten people in the world share a net wealth that is 1.5 times the national income of the world's least developed countries, home to 750 million people. At the same time, one third of the population of the developing countries — 1.3 billion people

— struggle to survive on less than $1 a day, and the numbers of poor people continue to grow.

Inequalities between developed and developing worlds, and within societies, mean that poverty is being reduced more slowly than is necessary if the international commitment, made at the United Nations Social Summit in 1995, to halving the incidence of poverty by 2015 is to be achieved. Inequality has two effects on poverty levels: it slows economic growth, and it makes a given rate of economic growth less effective in reducing poverty. While equity and economic growth are mutually reinforcing, inequality is socially destabilising, bad for growth, and of its nature restricts the capabilities of marginalised groups. Conversely, equitable access to markets, political power, and social provision, on the basis of needs, is the fastest and most effective route to poverty eradication. So there are moral *and* economic cases for growth with equity. For example, successful land-reform programmes have shown that, in terms of production costs and resource allocation, smallholder farming is highly efficient. More equal societies are also more likely to foster entrepreneurial behaviour, and less likely to generate rentier elites. And more equal societies are likely to invest more heavily in 'human capital'.

Recent trends in the distribution of wealth call for a renewed commitment to equitable development, which is clearly directed towards improving human well-being. This will require both a more even distribution of assets and opportunities than exists at present, and for more resources to be committed to national and international poverty-eradication strategies. The issue of how to mobilise resources for poverty eradication, or 'development finance', is a crucial one for states and for civil society, and will be considered later in the book. At present, most of the world's poorest countries lack the resources to meet the basic needs of the majority of their people.

Yet there is nothing inevitable about under-funding and under-provision of development strategies in poor countries. The fact that many poor countries have achieved marked improvements in living standards at low cost reinforces the point that determining the size and distribution of available resources, the 'resource envelope', is in large part a political decision. This is nowhere better illustrated than by the failure of the peace dividend since the end of the Cold War to support poverty eradication. If the resources mobilised in the 1980s by the industrial powers in a bid for geo-political supremacy had been matched in the 1990s by an equally concerted bid to eradicate absolute poverty, the task before us today would not appear so daunting.

Two clear challenges face the world at the beginning of the twenty-first century. First, to achieve sustained economic growth; and second, to realise the potential developmental gains of that growth. These two objectives must be pursued simultaneously if poverty eradication is to be achieved. As recent history in much of East Asia demonstrates, distributional, environmental, and political concerns cannot be postponed until growth has taken place, if improvements in material well-being are going to be sustainable. A proactive strategy on the part of the state is needed to ensure that growth with equity takes place, delivering lasting development to the millions of people who are currently denied it.

Definitions of poverty

Being clear at the outset about what we mean when we talk about poverty is crucial to establishing criteria of success and failure for any poverty-eradication strategy. Defining poverty is not simply, or primarily, a semantic exercise. Rather, it is an instrument of action. Yet definitions of poverty vary widely, and are often used interchangeably. Any discussion about poverty, and poverty eradication, needs to begin with agreement on the definitions, or discourse, being used.

Most commonly, 'poverty' refers to income poverty, and 'the poor' are those people living below an income line. Similarly, a poor country is one that has a low average per capita Gross National Product (GNP). But it is simplistic to see poverty as being determined only by low income. While there is a strong correlation between income and human-development indicators, income poverty does not fully account for low human development. While most high-income countries have high levels of human development, and most low-income countries have low levels of human development, there are plenty of exceptions: wealthy countries which have failed to distribute the benefits of economic growth equitably, and poor countries which have been remarkably successful in using limited resources equitably and efficiently. Some examples are discussed below.

Therefore, while income is closely associated with human development, other factors are involved in determining levels of human development. GNP growth is a measure of production income and expenditures, *not* the standard of living, which covers a broader range of goods, including good health, education, and social inclusion. GNP is only a partially useful indicator of the standard of living, because money is only one means by which we meet our needs. An important conclusion to draw from this is that poverty eradication is not simply about shunting x% of the population over an arbitrarily defined income-based line.

Instead of being measured by per capita GNP, which in fairness was never designed to be used as an indication of human well-being, poverty is best defined as *the state of being in which we are unable to meet our needs*. However, 'needs' are not simply the basic material necessities for subsistence. So the concept of 'needs' includes the notion of what is conventionally regarded as necessary to lead one's life as an integrated member of a particular society. In short, poverty is dynamic. Need is defined very differently across different cultures and generations, as technology and changing values alter perceptions of the prerequisites of an acceptable standard of living.

In *The Wealth of Nations*, Adam Smith, the eighteenth-century Scottish economist, recognised the importance of this point when he defined the ability to appear in public 'without shame' as a major criterion of individual human welfare.[2] To take an example from our own time, in Los Angeles the capacity to meet one's basic needs probably necessitates owning a car and an answer-phone, since without these commodities one is likely to have great difficulty either competing in the labour market or getting access to basic services. In rural Mozambique, a sufficient plot of cultivable land and access to a local market may be the basis of economic viability and a major determinant of social inclusion.

Basic needs extend beyond material goods to include intangibles such as the need to be valued, or treated with dignity, or to be free to participate politically, culturally, and economically in one's society. Commodities such as money are by and large means by which we are able to meet those needs. Jean Drèze and Amartya Sen have defined poverty in terms of constraints on capabilities (the freedom to achieve or meet our needs) and functionings (those things we want or need to achieve).[3] Poverty eradication, therefore, is best approached as an exercise in raising people's capabilities, or enhancing freedoms. The corollary of this approach to development is that empowerment — helping people in poverty to acquire the tools they need to meet their needs — is the long-term solution to poverty.

Of course, our ability to meet our needs changes, and is dependent on a range of variables such as health, climate, the state of the wider economy, and the level of corruption in government. This means that 'the poor' are a constantly changing and heterogeneous group of people, moving across a spectrum of relative degrees of welfare and deprivation, rather than comprising a monolithic section of society. For example, people in poverty move further below the poverty line in times of drought or conflict, when meeting basic needs suddenly becomes more difficult than was previously the case. In some societies, where a large proportion of the population lives close to the poverty line, even minor economic downturns or upturns can lead to dramatic changes in poverty levels. For example, in every Latin American country except Argentina and Uruguay, between 10 and 15% of the population live on incomes of between 0.9 and 1.25 times the value of the poverty line.[4] That the proportion of people *vulnerable* to poverty is greater than the total number of people currently living in poverty draws attention to the need for poverty-eradication strategies to address the vulnerabilities of the 'non-poor', as well as the vulnerabilities of people living in poverty.

Market liberalisation in an African country undergoing an International Monetary Fund structural adjustment programme captures another dimension of the relationship between poverty and external variables. While market liberalisation may benefit smallholder farmers who have access to storage facilities and good roads, poverty reduction among this group of farmers may be partially or fully offset by rising poverty among smallholder farmers for whom the loss of state purchasing arrangements has left them vulnerable to low prices from a single buyer – a condition known as monopsony.[5] This case illustrates a second important lesson for policy makers: when poverty rises, or falls, it is not necessarily rising or falling for every social or regional group. Positive aggregate trends often mask the negative experiences of particular social groups.

Institutions and poverty

Our ability to meet our basic needs depends not only on external variables, but also on our position in society. All societies differentiate between people by gender, class, caste, age group, religion, ethnicity, and race. These differentiations imply a hierarchy of opportunity, and the ability of a person to meet his or her basic needs is heavily influenced by an inherited 'opportunity set' based on the social groups to which he or she belongs. Aggregate approaches to poverty conceal these inequalities. For example, an indigenous child in the southern Mexican state of Chiapas is twice as likely to die before the age of five as is a child in Mexico City, 50% less likely to complete a primary education, and ten times more likely to live in a house without running water. This 'opportunity set' of the Chiapas child translates in adulthood into starkly different employment opportunities and wage levels: a child born in the wealthy northern state of Nuevo Leon will enter a labour market on leaving school that offers average wages almost double those in the south.[6] Therefore, policy makers are required to learn a third lesson: the 'capability constraints' of disadvantaged social groups need to be understood and challenged if poverty eradication is to take place.

The most disadvantaged social groups in a society, such as lower-caste widows in India, face capability constraints on two fronts: firstly, in securing an income; and secondly in converting that income into 'functionings' — those things that they want or need to achieve. This is because economic outcomes in India are mediated by overlapping gender and caste relations. Low-caste women have very limited access to education; widows (and low-caste widows especially) have little access to credit and labour markets; widows are usually unable to re-marry, and this increases vulnerability; and a woman does not usually inherit her husband's property.[7] There is a complex set of institutional factors underlying the widow's poverty, and eradicating poverty requires these institutional biases – whether related to labour markets or the education system or marriage laws — to be overcome. Institutions reflect the interests of more powerful and vocal social groups, and equity requires a shift in power relations as well as resources.

Inequalities within households illustrate the importance of addressing institutional biases as part of any poverty-eradication strategy. Traditionally economists have assumed that households are single-preference actors — in other words, that a household makes decisions about the allocation of time and resources in the same way as an individual does, rather than as a group of individuals with their own (often conflicting) needs and preferences.[8] This approach fails to acknowledge the bias in the intra-household division of labour, or in the distribution of household resources. The unequal distribution of household resources has important implications for poverty-eradication strategies, in that poverty is often concealed within a household that is above the poverty line.

This is clearly seen where women enter the labour market. Often the division of labour within the household remains unchanged, or household tasks are shifted on to other females in the household, because domestic tasks are seen as 'women's work'. This can effectively double the workload of women. Women's participation in labour markets tends to accelerate during economic downturns, which are associated with cuts in public provision of basic services. The burden of meeting basic needs then tends to be transferred from the state back to women and girls in the household. Often girls are withdrawn from education, or forgo other basic services as a result of these public disinvestments, and gender-based inequalities are thereby perpetuated.

The bias in the intra-household use of resources is reflected in health and nutrition outcomes and in mortality rates. There is evidence in many countries of widespread gender discrimination in the allocation of food and access to health care at the household level. In the Indian state of Uttar Pradesh, with a population the size of Brazil's, there are 879 females to every 1,000 males, and the life expectancy for women is two years lower than that for men. Even more starkly, supposing India had the same male–female ratio as sub-Saharan Africa, then 37 million 'missing women' would be added to its current population.[9] Both these cases illustrate the importance for sustained poverty eradication of overcoming institutional biases. At present, markets operate as if children are a private household investment, rather than both a public and private responsibility, forcing many poor households to adopt a 'short-term savings' approach towards children — and especially girls – for example by withdrawing them from school to contribute directly or indirectly to household income.

The importance of growth for development

Although economic growth is not a sufficient condition for sustained development, there are good reasons for focusing on wealth-creation as a necessary condition of development. Countries with the highest per capita incomes have, by most measures, the highest living standards. In the affluent 'developed' countries of the North, children are on average healthier, women are dramatically less likely to die in childbirth, people live longer lives, are more mobile and literate, and are widely perceived to enjoy more economic and social choice than the average person in the developing countries of the South. The wealth that has been generated in the industrial countries through sustained growth has funded these huge improvements in living standards, and this has fed back into the growth process. Advances in education and health contributed to productivity increases, with healthy and educated workers better able to work cooperatively and precisely, and to adapt to new technologies. The surplus generated by growth, and the effective investment of that surplus, created a virtuous circle of demand-led job-creating growth.

This happened in South Korea, where, in the space of two generations, heavy investment in social services, physical infrastructure, and technological upgrading transformed an overwhelmingly illiterate, agricultural society into a high-income industrialised country. High rates of per capita economic growth in particular allowed *absolute* increases in per capita social expenditure, without a *proportionate* increase in the burden on public or private spending.

Conversely, economic stagnation or negative growth shrinks the revenue base and reduces private incomes, threatening advances made in human development, and making improvements in living standards difficult to achieve. The formerly socialist 'transition' economies, whose one great achievement was their universal provision of health care and education, have witnessed an especially dramatic deterioration in health indicators since the post-liberalisation collapse in per capita incomes. Russia's male life expectancy, at 58 years, is now lower than that for India or Bolivia. Countries such as Zimbabwe, which has experienced negative per capita growth rates since 1980, have been hard pressed to maintain existing levels of spending on social provision and physical infrastructure, and health and education have suffered. Zimbabwe was one of sub-Saharan Africa's post-independence success stories in social provision, with marked improvements in school enrolment, literacy rates, and child mortality after 1980. Yet improvements in welfare have either slowed down — for example in reducing child mortality — or they have been reversed, as in life expectancy.

Falls in per capita income also make it more difficult for the poor to meet their basic needs in the market, and nutrition and housing quality tend to deteriorate, making people more vulnerable to illness and less productive economically. This means that even where, as in Cuba, governments protect social-expenditure levels despite economic collapse, public health will still suffer. Food shortages and a poor housing stock have increased the prevalence of communicable disease, while medical staff, unable to survive on their salaries, are forced to spend time away from their jobs, supplementing their incomes on the black market. For the first time since revolutionary health care took effect, child malnutrition has reappeared on a significant scale in Cuba; meanwhile, absentee teachers doubling up as petty traders hold back the learning of children.[10]

Economic growth is insufficient

Yet, despite the importance of economic growth in facilitating improvements in living standards, economic growth will not *automatically* deliver improved living standards. The way in which growth is distributed among a population will decide how effective it is in eradicating poverty and raising living standards. Unless policies which promote equitable distribution of the benefits and costs of growth are implemented, development will not follow.

The physical and human capital with which we enter the market largely determines the gains we receive. This means that unchecked growth, based on an initial highly unequal distribution of resources, will deliver highly unequal outcomes. Indeed, in most markets those entering with the largest stock of capital gain most proportionately, so that economic growth in very unequal societies tends to widen and entrench disparities. Unless equality of opportunity is actively pursued — through universal social provisioning and redistributive policies — welfare improvements will be slow and uneven, and development will be hard to achieve.

The case of Brazil illustrates this. An annual average GNP growth rate of 6.3% between 1965 and 1980 failed to make the inroads into poverty that it could have done, because access to resources and social provision was so grossly unequal. While human-development indicators improved and income poverty fell, in 1996 some 46 million people — close to 30 per cent of the population — were living in poverty, in the world's eighth largest economy. Each year, almost a quarter of a million Brazilian children die before reaching the age of 5 from illnesses which a clean water supply and adequate nutrition would prevent. Meanwhile, inequality in Brazil has widened still further. Today, Brazil's distribution of income and assets is more unequal than in the late 1970s, which applies a further brake on poverty reduction.[11]

In Brazil the pursuit of economic-growth goals obscured the need for economic stability and greater equality. The result was that growth in Brazil proved to be unsustainable. The economic downturn since 1980 has not yet been convincingly halted, with per capita incomes lower today in real terms than they were in the early 1980s. Inequality and poverty continue to restrict growth in Brazil, as years of under-investment and neglect of basic services have caught Brazilian industry in a medium-technology trap, with stagnating productivity levels.

While most East Asian countries have fared better than countries in Latin America in efforts to convert growth into opportunities for the poor, even here the relationship between growth and poverty reduction has often been weak. Both in Thailand, where the incidence of poverty in rural areas rose during a period of high growth between 1990 and 1995, and in China, where marginalised groups such as retrenched female workers have failed to benefit from the creation of new wealth, the impact of high growth rates has been anything but miraculous for millions of people. Clearly, poverty eradication depends both on economic growth and on public action to ensure that opportunities are distributed equitably. Growth can as easily undermine human development as it can support it. Inequality, environmental degradation, and social instability can all generate growth, but they will not deliver development. As the 1996 UNDP *Human Development Report* noted, policy makers need to be constantly aware of what sort of growth they are promoting. Is growth creating viable livelihood opportunities for poor people? Is growth based on environmentally unsustainable depletion of natural resources (and therefore contributing to intergenerational inequalities, by failing to sustain opportunities for future generations)? Is growth based on the exploitation of vulnerable groups, especially children? Clearly, the *quality* of the growth being promoted is crucial to its effectiveness in reducing poverty.

The challenge in a world of growing inequalities is to direct growth to the benefit of the poor as well as the rich. States must play a central part in this challenge: they can make a positive difference to people's standard of living by mobilising and allocating resources, and by regulating markets in the interests of the majority of people, so that they function as something more than a battleground for the pursuit of self-interest.

Table 1.1 Per capita income, inequality, and income poverty

(Sources: UNICEF, *State of the World's Children 1997;* UNDP, *Human Development Report 1996;* World Bank, *World Development Indicators 1997)*

Country	GNP per capita (US$)	Ratio between top and bottom income quintiles	Percentage of population in income poverty
Mexico	4180	13.6	14.9
Malaysia	3140	11.7	15.2
South Africa	3040	19.2	23.7
Brazil	2970	32.1	28.7
Botswana	2800	16.4	34.7
Indonesia	880	4.9	14.5
China	530	6.5	15.0
Zimbabwe	500	15.6	41.0

The role of distribution in poverty eradication

Because it is possible for income poverty to be reduced and for inequalities to rise simultaneously, it is often claimed that distribution and poverty eradication are separate concerns. For proponents of this view, poverty reduction is simply a function of growth and efficiency gains; what matters is not inequality *per se*, but economically adverse distributional outcomes: namely the effect of distribution on output and growth. If it can be demonstrated that concentrating 90 per cent of a country's productive resources in the hands of ten per cent of its people leads to 'optimal' outcomes (in other words, that *any* departure from the existing distribution would lead to less efficient production or allocation), then such a distribution is economically desirable.[12]

Yet the distribution of income, productive assets, and public spending all have an impact on poverty levels. Where incomes are more evenly distributed, the numbers of people living below the poverty line decrease. This can be seen in Table 1.1, by comparing China and Zimbabwe. The two countries have closely similar income levels. But whereas China is one of the more equal developing countries, Zimbabwe is highly unequal, with an average income among the wealthiest 20% which is 15 times higher than among the poorest 20%. The result is that Zimbabwe has income-poverty levels more than twice China's. Alternatively, if China had the same incidence of income poverty as Zimbabwe, then an additional 300 million Chinese people would be living in poverty. Contrary to the claim that distribution and poverty eradication are separate concerns, distributional issues need to be at the heart of any development strategy, both in terms of the initial distribution of productive opportunities, and in terms of the way that the wealth generated is used to secure public goods.

Income

Distribution of income is closely related to the extent and nature of poverty. Where there is a low average level of income, as is the case in most developing countries, the level of income inequality will be reflected in the incidence of income poverty, and in the 'poverty-reduction elasticity of growth', which captures the relationship between the level of inequality in a society and the amount of poverty reduction that a given growth rate will achieve. The lesson from Table 1.1 is clear: a more equal distribution of resources reduces poverty levels, and governments that are committed to poverty eradication need to implement redistributive policies. Even minor changes in the distribution of resources can have a considerable impact on poverty figures. The World Bank's 1990 *World Development Report* claimed that the redistribution of a mere 0.7% of Latin America's regional GDP could raise the income of every Latin American above the poverty line. This would be the equivalent of a two per cent tax on the wealthiest 20 per cent of the region's population. However, Latin American governments — in common with governments in much of the developing world — tend to tax regressively, taking a greater proportion of the income of the poor than they do of the rich. Regressive taxes have a disproportionate impact on the purchasing power of the poor, hitting directly their ability to meet their basic needs.

Assets

Income inequalities generally reflect asset inequalities. Unequal access to land, to technology, to outside markets, and to credit are all major factors in the extent and depth of poverty. Human capital – the skills acquired through education, for example – is another key asset that influences levels of poverty and inequality. The close relationship between asset and income inequality can be seen in the fact that those countries with the most unequal income distribution tend to have highly unequal land distribution. Brazil, where the ratio of the income-share of the wealthiest 20 per cent to the income-share of the poorest 20 per cent is 32, has a land-ownership Gini coefficient of 0.85 — the Gini coefficient measuring the departure from a theoretical state of perfect equality at 0 towards 1 – which is among the highest in the world.[13] Despite the accelerating demographic trend towards urbanisation in most countries of the South, the majority of the world's poor depend, directly or indirectly, on land for their survival. Poverty continues to be at its most extreme and pervasive in rural areas, and effective rural poverty eradication depends on land reform in most of Latin America, and parts of Africa and East Asia, where access to land is biased in favour of powerful elites. There is a close relationship between unequal access to land, low productivity, high levels of poverty, and rural violence. Improving access and opportunity for the poor may also depend on redistributing land in cities — where insecure tenure is a problem for millions of poor households — as well as in rural areas. Where carefully implemented, the short-term efficiency costs of land redistribution are fairly small, and in the long term smallholder farming can bring substantial efficiency gains.[14] Preferential or directed microfinance schemes, the development of intermediate technologies which lead to productivity gains, and infrastructural developments which improve market access for the poor are all potential poverty-reduction measures. Similarly, improved health and education outcomes among poor people raise their human-capital stock and tend to reduce income disparities, especially where – as in much of East Asia – economic growth is both labour-intensive and skills-intensive.

Public spending

The way in which public money is spent is a major determinant of poverty levels and the speed with which extreme poverty is eradicated. Government revenues are finite, and misallocation of scarce resources carries opportunity costs for the poor, as well as direct costs. For example, in Pakistan, the central government's social budget is one tenth that of its military budget. In a country with the unhappy distinction of having almost ten soldiers to every one doctor, three quarters of a million children under the age of five die every year from preventable diseases.[15]

Even where large sums of money are allocated by governments to social provision, poor health and educational outcomes often follow. The relationship between overall social-sector expenditure and welfare indicators is fairly weak. The principal influences on social outcomes are the cost-effectiveness of services and the extent to which access for the poor is prioritised. Total private and public per capita expenditure on health services in Brazil is almost 15 times that in China, yet child mortality is higher and life expectancy is lower.[16] Redistributive public spending is important to the poor, because health and educational inequalities are the major determinants both of economic inequality and social inequality. The costs of inequality are social as well as economic: our capacity to live as integrated members of a society is contingent not only on income, but also on our ability to participate politically and culturally, which among other things depends on good health, and equal access to information and literacy.

The relationship between inequality and growth

The costs of inequality

- ■ *Social cohesion* Social instability is often a response to levels of inequality rather than to poverty *per se*, and there appears to be a close correlation between conspicuous consumption by wealthy elites, high poverty levels, and a high incidence of violence. In countries as diverse as South Africa, the USA, and Russia, high or rising inequalities and high or rising rates of violent crime seem to be correlated. In many of the former centrally planned 'transition' economies, resentment of the conspicuous wealth of the new rich, and doubts over the methods used to acquire it, have eroded respect for the rule of law.[17] In Russia the effects of inequality on social cohesion are readily apparent. Corruption is endemic and the incidence of domestic violence, alcoholism, and homicides has increased markedly in the wake of the weakly regulated market liberalisation of the early 1990s.[18] Many East Asian countries have traditionally had low levels of inequality, and have placed considerable value on social cohesion. A year before violence forced political change in Indonesia, the World Bank cited anecdotal reports of a lower tolerance of income inequality than in other regions. Recession and widespread hardship in the wake of the financial crisis left people less willing to tolerate the extravagant lifestyle of the political elite, and growing disparities between rich and poor.[19]

■ *Economic costs* Social tensions and violent crime arising from inequality carry costs that are economic as well as social, as demonstrated by the loss of investor confidence in Indonesia following violence and political upheaval in 1998. The World Bank has estimated that in highly unequal countries such as Colombia, Jamaica, Brazil, and Mexico, with exceptionally high homicide rates, crime is taking one to two per cent off the growth rate each year.[20] Unequal societies tend to grow more slowly than unequal societies (see Figures 1.1 and 1.2), with extreme inequalities in income tending to discourage entrepreneurial behaviour and create rentier elites, who live off their assets and plough little of their wealth back into productive, job-creating investments. Inequality also encourages inefficient public-spending patterns which favour already privileged groups. Exchange-rate over-valuation is another common feature of unequal societies; particularly in Latin America during the 1980s, over-valued exchange rates were a commonly used device for reducing the cost of luxury imports enjoyed by elites.

■ *Political costs* The political costs of inequality are similarly high. Economic power is a major determinant of political power, and in highly unequal societies there are usually low levels of political participation. The economically disenfranchised are usually politically disenfranchised. In the USA, where voter turnout in presidential elections is little over 50 per cent, the welfare of the poorest ten per cent of Americans — among whom voter turnout is lowest – is rarely a contested political issue in mainstream national politics. Because imbalances in economic and political power are mutually reinforcing, unequal societies tend to generate populist political cultures, characterised by policy swings to 'buy off' vocal constituencies. Under these circumstances, states can become vehicles for patronage, with powerful sectional interests exploiting policies ostensibly intended to benefit the poor, and turning them instead to political ends. This happened with the PRONASOL social programme in Mexico, introduced in 1989 as a comprehensive response to persistently high poverty levels. By 1992, only one third of the programme's resources was explicitly directed to poverty alleviation. Increasingly, the ruling PRI government used the programme to buy political support.[21]

In contrast, low levels of inequality reduce imbalances and possible abuses of political power, and promote cooperative behaviour and the identification of collective goals. Sustainable prosperity depends on stability, and that stability depends in turn on equity. Conversely, income and asset inequalities contribute to cynicism about political processes and fragmentation in social relations. This risks reducing the market and political system to battlegrounds for the pursuit of crude self-interest. Such a scenario is unlikely to deliver sustainable and equitable growth.

Growth and equity: the myth of a trade-off

The debate on growth and distribution has been dominated by economists who see development as involving inevitable trade-offs between economic growth and equity, and, implicitly, between the welfare of competing social groups. Despite the widespread evidence that extreme inequality is bad for growth and poverty reduction, liberal economists — beginning with Simon Kuznets in the 1950s — have influentially argued that developing societies, especially during economic 'take-off', face two choices. They must opt either for a highly theoretical state of optimal economic efficiency, or for socially desirable outcomes, since there is a trade-off in *efficiency* terms between the two.

Two distinct arguments can be identified. First, that growth generates inequalities in the medium term, and that this is a necessary condition, given the need for accumulated capital to fill the savings gap (the shortfall between the amount a society saves and the amount it needs for investment) in emerging economies. Second, that any attempts to equalise the growth process will carry considerable efficiency costs and slow down the growth process. Neither of these arguments is borne out by empirical studies, yet they continue to be employed as a rationale for economic policies that create and perpetuate inequalities.

Contrary to the liberal arguments on growth and efficiency, there is a body of evidence that suggests that, economically as well as socially, inequality carries considerable efficiency costs, and that there is a positive synergy between growth and equity. Firstly, there is no evidence of rapid growth necessarily generating inequality, as was widely argued in the 1980s. Rapid growth since 1945, both in Europe and East Asia, has seen the distribution of resources becoming *more* rather than less equal, as growth has proceeded apace.[22] Second, there is plentiful evidence that inequality is a brake on growth, and that unequal access to land in particular hampers economic development.[23] In the developing world, the fastest growing economies are generally the most equal: Figure 1.1 (overleaf) reveals the relationship between GNP per capita growth over a 25-year period — long enough to account for any short-term fluctuations — for a broad range of developing countries, set against the ratio of the income-share of the top income quintile to that of the bottom income quintile. While there are some notable exceptions (Botswana's combination of high income inequality and high growth, and India and Pakistan's record of relative equality and weak growth), there is no evidence that there is any necessary relation between high growth and inequality.

There also appears to be a close relationship between high levels of wage inequality, poor labour relations, and low productivity. Labour-productivity growth in the OECD from 1979 to 1990 has been lowest in those countries with the highest degrees of income inequality (see Figure 1.2). Productivity levels are highest where employees feel valued and respected, and enjoy their jobs; cooperative behaviour is less likely in workplaces with extreme wage differentials and conspicuous hierarchies. Nor do marked wage differentials appear to promote labour-market competition and income-group mobility, as is often suggested, with low-income workers recognising that the benefits of upgrading their skills outweigh the costs. Evidence from the USA and the UK, where wage differentials are both growing and the highest among the industrial economies, suggests that workers from low-income groups in flexible labour markets remain in low-paid jobs for much longer periods of time than do workers in more regulated economies.[24]

27

Figure 1.1 Developing-country distribution and growth 1970–1995
(*Source:* World Bank, *World Development Indicators 1997;* UNDP, *Human Development Report 1996*)

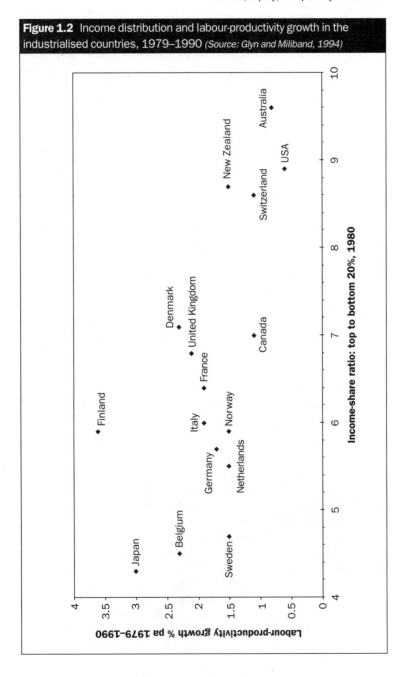

Figure 1.2 Income distribution and labour-productivity growth in the industrialised countries, 1979–1990 *(Source: Glyn and Miliband, 1994)*

In many ways, this is predictable. Firstly the poor are those people who suffer capability constraints; where market opportunities exist for those with saleable skills or knowledge, those with capability constraints are excluded. As a result, the poor have low productivity levels and contribute little to national income. High levels of poverty and inequality and low growth rates are mutually reinforcing; unless redistributive policies are adopted, including substantial investment in universal social provision, this cycle is unlikely to be broken.

Secondly, it has been suggested by some economists that extreme income inequality creates irresistible political pressures for inefficient redistributive policies, which slow down growth. While it is difficult to gauge the precise relationship between inequality and political choices, it does seem to be the case that societies with highly unequal income distribution, from Central America to Southern Africa, often have clientelistic power structures and weak participative political cultures. This encourages populist and inefficient redistributive measures, such as food subsidies, support of loss-making state enterprises which provide employment for the urban population, and one-off social programmes which have little impact on poverty levels. Entrenched political and economic elites are far more likely to co-opt potential opponents, such as trade unions and the armed forces, by redistributing on the margins, than implement a radical redistribution of productive assets.

The efficiency of growth

Finally, and perhaps most importantly, the more unequal the society, the higher the growth rate needed to achieve a given rate of poverty reduction. The relationship between the level of inequality in a society and how much poverty reduction is achieved by a given growth rate is known as the 'poverty-reduction elasticity of growth'. The slow pace of poverty reduction in Latin America is closely related to the region's uneven distribution of wealth and social opportunity. Conversely, the unprecedented growth rates in East Asia over the last three decades led to dramatic poverty reduction, because of the equitable distribution of economic opportunities. East Asia's 'miracle' growth rates up to the financial crisis in 1997 are well known, but they effected a transformation of the region that is less well appreciated. Between 1975 and 1995 the number of people in East Asia living below the poverty line more than halved, from more than 700 million to 345 million, over a period in which the population doubled.[25] In contrast, the numbers of income-poor in Latin America and South Asia increased over the same period, while sub-Saharan Africa witnessed both a proportionate and an absolute rise in the numbers of people below the poverty line. These huge inter-regional variations in the efficiency with which growth translates into poverty reduction are a reminder that the distribution of productive assets is as important for poverty eradication as is sustained economic growth.

The cases of some individual East Asian countries are even more remarkable. In the last decade, Chinese per capita incomes have doubled on the back of average growth rates of over 7%. In Britain, it took 60 years to achieve a comparable increase in income after the industrial revolution.[26] In South Korea in 1945, per capita incomes were lower than for Sudan, only 13% of the population could read and write, and the economy was in a ruinous state, with negligible sums of fixed investment and the vast majority of the population dependent on primitive farming for their survival.[27] Yet by 1997, absolute poverty had been virtually eradicated, life expectancy and child mortality rates were closely similar to Portugal's, and the country had industrialised and had joined the OECD. Despite the recent financial crisis, the lesson holds: rapid growth had released resources for poverty reduction, and made dramatic social improvements possible. But the *efficiency* with which growth translated into poverty reduction was the result largely of the initial distribution of productive assets, and the labour-intensive nature of the early stages of growth.

In Latin America, unequal income distribution means that growth rates several times faster than those recorded by Korea over three decades would be needed to achieve Korean poverty-reduction rates. Mexico's poverty-reduction elasticity of growth is so low that it would have to register a growth rate *four times* that of South Korea in order for the poorest tenth of Mexico's population to receive an increase in their incomes equivalent to that received by the poorest tenth in South Korea from each percentage point of growth. And whereas every dollar of growth generated in Indonesia increases the income of the poorest ten per cent by seven cents, in Brazil, for every dollar of wealth generated, the poorest decile receive only one cent. In other words, Brazil would need to grow at *seven times* the rate of Indonesia to achieve a comparable rate of poverty reduction.[28]

The fact that Latin America requires growth rates several times those achieved in East Asia if it is to achieve equally rapid poverty reduction is especially sobering, given its recent growth performance. Between 1990 and 1995, regional GDP growth averaged just over 3.2%, compared with 10.3% in East Asia. Given annual average population growth of 1.5%, per capita incomes have recovered only very slightly from the negative growth of the 1980s. Most Latin Americans today are no better off in real income terms than they were in the mid-1970s, and many Andean and Central American countries have lower per capita incomes today than in the late 1960s.

The low poverty-reduction elasticity of growth explains why poverty remains so stubbornly high in Latin America, despite the modest recovery of recent years. According to the Economic Commission for Latin America, the number of poor and indigent people in the region actually rose from 197 million to 209 million between 1990 and 1995.[29] Growth patterns in Latin America reflect asset distribution, and asset distribution is grossly unequal. Regionally, the income-share ratio between the highest and lowest income quintiles rose from ten in 1980 to 12 in 1990. In Brazil, between 1981 and 1990, a period of per capita income growth, the average incomes of the poorest 30% of the population fell in real terms, while the average income of the wealthiest 10% witnessed a rise of 20%.[30] Without a radical redistribution of assets, growth will continue to fail to make significant inroads into poverty.

The pattern of low growth or no growth, and of growth making little impact on poverty levels, is repeated in sub-Saharan Africa and South Asia, which between them account for close to 60 per cent of the world's income-poor. In sub-Saharan Africa, 220 million people are living on less than one dollar a day (the international poverty line), and in some countries, such as Madagascar, Niger, and Zambia, over 60 per cent of the population are defined as living below the poverty line. Since 1980, economic performance in the region has been abysmal, with a negative annual per capita growth rate of almost 1%. Despite some recent signs of incipient recovery, the optimism in some quarters about an 'African renaissance' seems misplaced. Even if per capita incomes rose by the projected World Bank figure of 1.3% over the next decade, incomes would have only reached early 1980s levels by 2007. The best-case scenario is that average incomes can be doubled over the next half century, reaching the current developing-country average in 2050 and still leaving perhaps one third of the population below the income-poverty line. As in Latin America, the relationship between growth and poverty reduction is a weak one. In the case of Zimbabwe, growth at twice the rate in Vietnam is needed for the bottom income decile to receive the same increase in income. And Kenya would need growth at double the rate in Thailand in order for the poorest ten per cent to receive a commensurate rise in income.[31]

In South Asia, home to more than half a billion of the world's poorest people, recent economic growth has made limited impact on income-poverty levels. In India, economic liberalisation in the early 1990s broke the 'Hindu rate of growth' of under 4% a year which had characterised post-independence India, and output has recently been rising at a more 'tigerish' 6% a year. Yet because of the forms that growth has taken, excluding swathes of village India, significant inroads have not been made into income poverty. Absolute numbers below the poverty line have risen, and between 1990 and 1994 the proportion of income-poor fell by only 1%, from 36% to 35% of the population.[32]

Redistribution on the margin, or redistribution of assets?

There are compelling moral and economic objections to be made to the marked inequalities of income and assets discussed above. Unchecked distributional outcomes are neither efficient nor meritocratic, since they primarily reflect inherited opportunities. If people enter the market as highly unequal participants, they will exit with highly unequal gains, with the initially privileged likely to consolidate their advantage, because of their access to capital, information, and social networks.

The relationship between growth and distribution, and the role of redistributive policies in fostering growth, has been debated vigorously since the 1950s, when the economist Arthur Lewis emphasised the importance of steady increases in per capita income to political stability.[33] Distributional issues were largely ignored, and it was taken for granted that growth would benefit the whole of society, even if some people benefited more than others. Indeed, it was widely regarded as inevitable that economic development would lead in the short run to greater income inequality. This was claimed to be both a result of the shift from traditional sectors of the economy – especially agriculture – to higher-productivity modern sectors such as manufacturing, and a result of the need for savings accumulation (and therefore a greater concentration of wealth) to finance investments in industries with higher added value.

Yet, despite unprecedented growth rates in the developing world during the 1950s and 1960s, there was growing evidence by the mid-1970s that rapid growth was failing to reduce poverty levels substantially. Growth in many Latin American countries in particular was concentrated in capital-intensive industries, with the result that income inequalities widened and under-employment rose. And in Asia a seven-country study, undertaken by the ILO, revealed widespread falls in the income of the rural poor, against a backdrop of per capita GDP growth.[34] The failure to convert fast growth into fast poverty reduction forced a rethink of development strategies on the part of governments and international organisations. In 1974 the World Bank published a study calling for 'redistribution with growth', proposing marginal redistribution of the benefits of growth. Yet redistribution remained a *post hoc* strategy, a way of moderating the distributional effects of unequal growth, and discussion of asset distribution was largely bypassed.[35] The study failed to consider the political feasibility of annual transfers from the upper 60% to the lower 40% income group that it proposed, and the poor were treated as a homogeneous bloc, with no thought given to the likely impact of redistributive policies on particular social groups.

The failure of incremental redistributive policies of the sort proposed by the World Bank to achieve rapid and substantial poverty reduction where large asset-inequalities persist, and a growing literature on the growth and equity benefits of asset redistribution in Taiwan and South Korea, have strengthened the case for 'redistribution before growth'. For governments committed to improving distributional outcomes through a market-based economy, the key question is whether equality of opportunity is best achieved by redistributing productive assets or by redistributing on the margin — redistributing income from the richer to the poorer people in a society, either directly, or through investment strategies designed to benefit the poor, such as basic health care, housing, or primary education.

Redistribution on the margins, in the form of measures such as food subsidies for the poor, rent controls, and a minimum wage, has often been regarded by governments as less politically risky than the redistribution of productive assets, such as land. For this reason, marginal redistributive policies have been widely and ineffectively used where income and asset inequalities have been most marked: in Latin America and in Southern Africa. There is no evidence that these sorts of measure, even where well implemented, have a significant equalising effect. Indeed, there is widespread evidence that populist measures in highly unequal societies tend to be growth-retarding.[36] Redistribution on the margins can carry efficiency costs, not all of them borne by privileged groups: minimum-wage laws can be inflationary, and can encourage the use of labour-saving technologies; rent controls can lead to under-investment and a shortfall in rented housing stock; and so on. The bureaucracies that are often created by such market controls can themselves be a drain on public resources and have a disequalising effect. In the case of redistributing on the margin through investment strategies, 'leakage' is a particular problem. Feeder roads and irrigation subsidies cannot often be targeted precisely at the very poor, and often the poorest — being assetless — fail to derive any benefit from this sort of investment.

While pro-poor investments, especially in the social sectors, are a vital component of poverty-eradication strategies, they will not succeed alone. Tackling inequality solely at the level of income, especially in countries where wages account for a small proportion of average household income, is misplaced. Income levels are more a symptom than a cause of inequalities — of asset distribution, educational attainment, market access, and political power. The redistribution of productive assets, particularly land, has in contrast been shown to have considerable potential benefits in terms of reducing poverty and inequality, and raising efficiency and growth levels.

Building equitable growth: some key lessons

Directed development, of which redistributive policies are a part, requires a strong state administrative capacity. It is clear that this is missing in many developing countries, which is a major factor in the conspicuous failure of so many states to support development. However, 'state failure' is not a justification of the claims made for the allocative efficiency of the market. Instead of rendering the state irrelevant, globalisation has led to new demands being made on the state to develop new markets and provide high-quality public services. At the same time, the costs of state failure are rising, as countries are placed in increasing competition with one another for finite sums of foreign investment.

The idea that development is primarily a spontaneous process is historically unfounded and inherently implausible. All states — even 'nightwatchman' states restricted to providing only the most basic regulatory framework for the market — need policies, and at the least they have a role to play in supporting markets.[37] Historically, from nineteenth-century post-unification Germany to Taiwan under nationalist rule, states have been agents of developmental change in two major ways. Firstly, through the extension of social provision, and in particular literacy and health services. And secondly, through the establishment and support of industries and economies of scale, and the shaping of competitive advantage.

In both cases, finite resources dictate that states must take into account distributional considerations. Every policy intervention by every state implicitly acknowledges that the market mechanism, unchecked, will not deliver optimal distributive outcomes. If growth is not an end in itself, as Aristotle observed, there is a need for collective choices about the ends to which it should be directed. These objectives are not necessarily obvious. Lengthening life expectancy in Mozambique is imperative in a way it is not in Britain, where enhancing the quality of life demands different priorities (for example, in the matter of pensions policy).[38] Identifying these objectives requires a critical examination of policy alternatives in the public arena. Equitable and sustainable development is necessarily participatory.

It follows from this that there are no development blueprints. There is much to emulate in the initiatives of the four East Asian 'tigers' (Hong Kong, Singapore, Korea, and Taiwan), whose development experience is discussed further in this book: their commitment to universal education and health provision, and their success in pursuing a labour-intensive growth strategy; but developing countries might find their mistakes equally instructive. This is particularly the case in the light of the IMF stabilisation programmes in East Asia, and the events, beginning with the forced devaluation of the Thai *baht*, that led up to them. The reverse side of East Asian growth is a history of weak financial regulation, petty authoritarianism, human-rights abuses, disregard for the environment, and state corruption.

While the East Asian financial crisis does not undermine the basic case for an activist state supporting social investment and labour-intensive industrial development strategies, it does illustrate the risks involved where there is a lack of political transparency and accountability. South Korea's giant corporations, or *chaebol*, are a case in point. They became overburdened with debt because of the habit of allocating funds according to political rather than economic criteria, and then covering up the true extent of the problem through an elaborate system of cross-subsidisation and creative accounting. The situation was further exacerbated by short-term overseas borrowing, in collusion with the government. While a proper discussion of the East Asian crisis is beyond the scope of this book, it does underline the need for development strategies to be rooted in public debate, participation, and learning.

The positive lesson demonstrated by the Asian tigers is that an activist state can convert rapid economic growth into effective and lasting poverty reduction, and the poor can produce and trade their way out of poverty. The lessons to be drawn from the region are especially important for sub-Saharan Africa, Latin America, and South Asia, where recent poverty-reduction and economic records have generally ranged from disappointing to disastrous, and hundreds of millions of people are daily denied their most basic rights to sufficient food, clean water, basic health care, and an education. Despite the broad range of policies pursued by the tigers,[39] three core commitments can be identified in the region:

- A recognition from the outset that universal social provision of a high quality is integral to a successful rapid-growth strategy. Public investment in education and health care created a workforce which was literate and healthy, and therefore equipped to adapt to new technologies.

- An activist commitment to equitable labour-intensive growth and workplace training, with rising labour productivity and wage levels feeding into a virtuous circle of rapid growth and social investment. Labour-intensive growth meant that a higher proportion of the population participated in the growth process, and the benefits of growth were widely shared.

- Close control of direct investment flows, with a focus on technology transfers in industries of high added value, and a gradualist approach to trade liberalisation. Investments were directed to 'strategic' industries producing high-value goods. Protection from foreign competition was given to infant industries, while successful firms were rewarded with state support, and failing firms were often shut down.[40]

In the wake of the financial crisis, the benefits of political control over investment in East Asia have been widely questioned. Some commentators have argued that political interference in markets lay at the heart of the crisis. Yet the most significant lesson to be drawn continues to be that governments that are committed to rapid growth need to commit themselves to equity. The following chapters discuss what the components of an equitable growth strategy might be. Public goods and livelihoods are examined in turn, with broad public-policy recommendations at the end of each chapter. The report concludes with a distillation of these recommendations.

2 Social investment

Getting the fundamentals right

Analysis of the East Asian development experiences has often emphasised the ways in which governments got 'the fundamentals' of macro-economic policy right. Whatever other policies they adopted, growth was ultimately grounded in a sound economic record — the control of inflation and public spending, and until recently, the avoidance of overvalued exchange rates — a record that was notably absent in most developing countries. Getting the fundamentals right generated wealth, increasing the purchasing power of the poor and the revenue-raising capacity of the state. Wealth creation was labour-intensive, both in agriculture and in industry, and this translated into rapid poverty reduction: very few millionaires were created, but very few of the poor were left behind. The moral to be drawn is that without a firm foundation for growth, poverty reduction and development will not follow.

Sound macro-economic policy is undoubtedly a necessary basis for sustained and rapid growth, but the focus on this dimension of East Asian development has often obscured an equally important basic policy priority in the region: the rapid expansion in social-service provision by public means in the crucial early phases of development. As these early investments fed into the growth process, and incomes rose, the role of the market in social provision expanded. Nonetheless, the role of the state, as both regulator and provider, remained central in the 'tiger economies'. The East Asian countries recognised that, whatever the private returns to social investment, the social and economic costs of leaving provision to chance in the market-place are prohibitively high.

In the most narrowly economic sense, a public good is a good that cannot be provided to a restricted clientele, and for which there is consequently limited private demand. An example might be a pest-control or clean-air programme, from which people are able to benefit whether or not they have paid for it. The outcome, of course, is that if it is left to the market mechanism, nobody pays for it. In such instances, the state is needed to deliver the good. There are few pure public goods, and very little health and education provision can be treated simply as such. For example, the individual captures many of the returns to an education — by raising his or her potential earnings – and the economic analysis of returns on investment in education has provided an influential rationale for introducing charges for some social services, particularly at the higher levels.[1] However, health and education, especially at the basic level, have a high 'public-goods content'. The social benefits of mass literacy or the eradication of smallpox are enormous, yet private demand is limited. Conversely, there is much higher private demand for expensive, curative health care and university education, since most of the returns are captured by the individual.

Traditionally, public provision of basic health care and education has been seen as desirable in terms of *efficiency* and *equity* objectives.[2] The principal objection on efficiency grounds to marketised provision is that health and education services benefit people other than the direct recipient, with these 'externalities' encouraging lower expenditures than are optimal in the absence of public provision. The equity costs of marketised provision are also considerable. Typically, private education or health care is beyond the means of the poorest households. Because education and health are powerful determinants of future income, private provision tends to strengthen existing income inequalities. Oxfam believes the benefits to society of providing good-quality basic health and education services for all are such that leaving basic social provision to the market, especially in poor countries, is counterproductive. At the basic level of education and health provision, the social rate of return is especially high, and the equity costs of marketising provision are considerable.

Social provision as a right and as investment in human capital

Human development is a good in itself and is good for growth. The relegation of social provision to the 'second tier' of policy priorities implies that only once the macro-economic basics are in place can social considerations be accorded a higher priority. Too often, social programmes are 'bolted on' to ameliorate some of the crueller effects of rapid growth on marginalised groups. This is misplaced: social provision is a catalyst for long-term growth and development. There is a mutually reinforcing effect between social investment and growth. Under-investment in health and education is a brake on growth, and slower growth means that fewer resources are available to invest in these public goods. A vicious circle of low growth or no growth, limited resources for social investment, and low productivity gains is often established, and many developing countries are caught in this trap.

Conversely, strong social investment and rapid growth can be mutually reinforcing, releasing further resources for investment which can improve the standard of living and strengthen the growth process. The East Asian experience demonstrates the catalytic effect of human-capital investment on growth, and the effective use of revenues to expand and improve public services. At the same time, education and health care cannot be treated as 'magic bullets'; the link between a country's endowments of human capital and growth is not automatic. What was important about the Asian experience was that the increased supply of skilled and healthy labour was matched by a demand from labour-intensive industries for skilled and healthy workers. In contrast, in countries such as Zimbabwe, despite heavy investment in basic social services, macro-economic mismanagement and capital-intensive production in agriculture have resulted in persistently high levels of underemployment and poverty. The next chapter will examine some of the policies needed to ensure that human-development strategies are linked to livelihood opportunities for the poor, and therefore to economic development. Nonetheless, the lesson is clear: getting the fundamentals right in social provision is a necessary condition of converting growth into development.

This is not to say that literacy and good health have only an instrumental value *vis à vis* GDP growth. Talk of 'human capital investment' can be useful in helping to focus on the relationship between a healthy and skilled workforce and productivity growth. But health and education are also basic rights, which have an intrinsic value, and which strengthen the ability of people to claim other rights.[3] Oxfam's experience of working with poor communities has shown that people place a value on good health and the opportunity to learn that exceeds their value as economic investments. Social provision contributes to some of the less immediately tangible goals of development, such as autonomy and self-respect, which do not have a marketable value. In short, access to good-quality social provision, clean water, and decent housing enhances well-being. Conversely, ill-health and ignorance severely constrain a person's capacity to play a full social and cultural role in the life of the community, and their significance as causes of poverty equals that of material deprivation. Adam Smith warned against the folly of judging a person solely by his or her usefulness, 'that for which we commend a chest of drawers'.[4]

Social investment and growth

So the basic rights to an education and health care are goods in themselves, enhancing the lives of people with access to them, and as such they are 'developmental'. But good-quality social provision is also essential to sustained growth. Universal social provision both benefits individuals who are currently denied it, and acts as a developmental catalyst as it starts to feed into the growth process. Whereas 50 years ago a developing country's competitive advantage was shaped largely by natural-resource endowments and labour costs, competitiveness in world markets is now based increasingly on levels of human capital and institutional stability. The industries with the highest added value are now knowledge-based, and the economic losers are those individuals and societies which fail to invest in their stock of human capital.

Education is the cornerstone of a productive workforce and growing economy. Literate adults are more adaptable and productive than non-literate ones in the formal job market, and an economy will succeed in climbing the value-added ladder only if skills are constantly upgraded, through both public-sector education and workplace training. Equipping the poor with the skills they need to adapt to new technologies, take up market opportunities, and generate wealth — rather than waiting for the benefits of wealth to trickle down to them — is the most just *and* the most effective route out of poverty. In East Asia the importance of this link between equitable access to social provision and poverty reduction was recognised early on, and universal social provision was from the outset an integral part of development strategies. In South Korea, universal social provision was achieved by the 1960s, anticipating future demand for skilled labour from technology-intensive industries and services. As early as 1960, Korean literacy rates stood at 70%, far above the rates in most South Asian and sub-Saharan African countries today. The Korean poor were far better equipped than the poor in Pakistan or Peru to work efficiently, accurately, and co-operatively in labour-intensive manufacturing, even before economic 'take-off'.

Comparing the educational record and productivity growth in East Asia and Latin America gives a clearer picture of the correlation between social provision and growth. As Table 2.1 shows, since the 1970s the East Asian region has overtaken Latin America, in terms of both education and productivity. In the last 15 years, per capita income has remained constant in Latin America, while productivity has stagnated. Although some Latin American countries enjoyed healthy growth rates up to 1980, years of under-investment in education and health created a labour bottleneck when Import-Substituting Industrialisation (ISI) policies were exhausted and there was a demand for new strategies enabling countries to move into industries with higher added value.

Table 2.1 Productivity and educational status: Latin America and East Asia
(*Sources:* IDB 1997; UNICEF, *State of the World's Children 1997*)

	Latin America	East Asia excl. China
GDP/worker (1995 US$)		
1975	8,800	5,300
1985	8,900	7,800
1992	8,900	11,800
% of children reaching grade 5		
in primary school 1995	73	87
Secondary-school enrolment ratio		
male	45	57
female	49	49

Whereas the more successful East Asian economies succeeded in attracting Foreign Direct Investment (FDI) in industries with high added value, on the basis of their human-capital levels, foreign investment in Latin America has been a mix of privatisation receipts, portfolio investment, and investment in construction and *maquiladora* (assembly) industries. The range of investments here reflects the interrelated low skill levels, state inefficiency, and poor infrastructure that characterise most countries in the region. Most Latin American countries have found themselves in a cycle of low human-capital investment, stagnating productivity, underemployment, and politically destabilising inequalities. But not all East Asian countries have maintained adequate investment in social provision either, and some countries in the region are feeling the effects of the medium-technology trap, as skills shortages have restricted growth in industries with higher added value. Both in Malaysia and Thailand, the rate of increase in demand for skills and education has outstripped supply, leading to widening wage differentials. This skills shortage has not only been disequalising, it has also led to foreign investors moving production offshore, and between 1992 and 1997 there was a slowdown in new manufacturing FDI entering Malaysia.[5]

Social provision, poverty reduction, and equality

Reducing poverty

By definition, effective social provision reduces poverty. Good health and literacy raise human capabilities, enhancing an individual's effective freedoms. Ill health is an obvious cause of poverty and a constraint on escaping from poverty, carrying both direct and opportunity costs. Poor health and disability are expensive for the sufferer and his or her household in terms of lost income, time spent caring by other household members, money spent on hospital visits, palliative care and medicines, and distress-sales of assets in order to finance these purchases. Illness is also expensive for an economy in terms of lost productivity. This is especially the case with conditions — such as HIV-AIDS — which tend to kill the economically productive section of the population, radically altering the dependency structure and demographic profile of whole societies, and destroying painstakingly developed human capital.[6]

The ability to secure a viable livelihood and escape poverty is heavily influenced by illness and disability. Chronic diseases such as schistosomiasis (bilharzia), which affects 200 million people in developing countries, often severely restrict the ability of sufferers to secure a livelihood, as do disabilities such as poor eyesight and cataracts that are not rectified. In conflict-scarred countries such as Cambodia, Angola, and Bosnia, injuries sustained as a result of stepping on landmines often result in poverty for whole households, as new dependants are created. For people with physical disabilities, who face institutional biases in markets, there are obstacles both to securing an income, and then to converting that income into functionings.

But even basic health measures demanding relatively modest resources can have a marked impact on poverty levels in a very short space of time. Health education, immunisation of children and pregnant women, the attendance of trained medical staff at births, adequate sanitation, improved housing stock, and, perhaps most importantly, clean water supplies — which the World Health Organisation estimates could by itself prevent 80 per cent of all sickness — can radically improve the quality of life for poor individuals and communities, and enhance their capacity to secure a viable livelihood. In the southern Indian state of Kerala, an average life expectancy of 74 years for women and 69 for men, and an infant mortality rate of 16 per thousand live births have been achieved with effectively and equitably targeted public-health expenditure, contributing to human-development levels similar to those in countries in the upper-middle income range.[7]

Equitable educational provision can similarly lead to spectacular improvements in the quality of life for the poor. Education has a pivotal role to play in any strategy designed to extend the range of income-earning opportunities for the poor. Illiteracy and low educational achievement translate into fewer opportunities to sell one's labour; in periods of economic downturn and high unemployment, the least educated are less likely to adapt to changing demands in the labour market or to find new employment opportunities. There is a strong connection between educational attainment and income poverty: in Mexico, three quarters of heads of households living below the poverty line have failed to complete a primary education, more than double the average completion rate among the adult population, while in Brazil the lowest income quintile's average length of attendance at school is 2.1 years, against 8.7 years for the highest quintile.[8] And in Thailand, the incidence of poverty among households headed by an uneducated person is twice the national average, and more than 50% higher than for households headed by a person with only a lower-primary schooling.[9]

The importance of education extends beyond raising average income levels and equipping the poor to lift themselves out of poverty. Illiteracy makes people more vulnerable to exploitation and less likely to have their needs reflected in the structure of institutions. A clear example of this vulnerability can be seen in labour markets, where illiterate workers are less likely to have a formal employment contract, more likely to be cheated of pay, and unlikely to be able to hold public authorities to account. The connection between illiteracy and a weakened position in labour markets is strongly affected by gender. Seventy per cent of the world's 900 million illiterate adults are women, and both in the developed and developing economies women's work is concentrated disproportionately in low-wage sectors. Partly because women are seen as less likely to organise themselves and press for improved working conditions than men, they are particularly attractive to employers in globally competitive export industries — such as textiles — where there is a strong downward pressure on wages. In Bangladesh, 85% of the country's one million textile workers are women, mostly working for 10 to 16 hours a day in Dhaka or Chittagong, where monthly pay of 500 *taka* — approximately £10 — is common.[10]

Extending educational opportunity is crucial for the empowerment of poor people at a number of levels. A literate person, able to think critically and able to articulate his or her interests coherently, is better able to participate meaningfully in political processes, whether at the household, community, or national level, than a person without any education. In this respect it is no coincidence that literacy rates in Tibet, at 45% for men and 25% for women, are so low in comparison with the Chinese provincial averages of 90% and 63% respectively.[11] Educational inequality perpetuates unequal access to the sources of political power, just as it perpetuates unequal access to income-earning opportunities.

Table 2.2 Education–fertility correlations in the state of Kerala and India
(*Sources:* Drèze and Sen *1995;* UNICEF, *State of the World's Children 1997)*

	Female literacy rate* 1990–1991	Fertility rate 1992	Infant mortality rate per 1,000 live births 1995
India	52	3.7	76
Kerala	98	1.8	16

* The literacy rate is for the 15-19 years age group.

The additional effects of equitable educational provision can be felt also at the more local level: for example, where a literate villager is able to read out an important news report on a health risk, or write to a politician requesting action on neglected local infrastructure. Educating girls has a marked effect on child health and household hygiene, and education and health provision have a complementary effect on each other. Healthy children are better able to concentrate and learn in the classroom, and literate adults tend to be more easily persuaded by health advice, are more likely to demand timely treatment, and are better able to gain access to and process information on health care. Conversely, ill health is an obstacle to effective learning. Common childhood illnesses in developing countries, such as diarrhoea, not only affect concentration and learning, but also lead to prolonged absences from school. Illness can have especially negative effects on girls' learning, since healthy girls are often withdrawn from school to care for sick family members.

Maternal education also is closely correlated with lower fertility rates. Table 2.2 shows the female literacy and fertility rates for the Indian state of Kerala and for India as a whole, demonstrating the close correlation between literacy, fertility, and child health. While some commentators have seen female education as a tool for population control, lower fertility rates are important principally because of the dangers to health and the quality of life that are posed to women and their children by frequent and unplanned pregnancies.[12] Freeing women from this burden can help to extend their range of opportunities to participate in public life. Unsurprisingly, women have a far greater public role in political, educational, and economic spheres in Kerala than they do elsewhere in India, and this has reinforced the progress in health and education indicators made in the state since Indian independence.[13]

Combating inequality

Extending social provision to the poor and socially marginalised can have an equalising effect on at least two fronts. First, education in particular can strengthen the political voice of marginalised groups, such as poor women or indigenous people — raising self-awareness and enhancing the ability to organise and articulate shared interests — and can establish a dynamic for institutional change. Second, equitable social provision can reduce income inequalities. Levels of wage inequality are closely related to educational status and, to a lesser extent, health status. According to the World Bank, differences in educational attainment and skills levels account for between one third and one half of variations in earnings across individuals within countries. While these findings should be treated as indicative, given the difficulty of controlling for social and institutional factors in econometric analysis, it is clear that the scarcer human capital is in any labour market, the higher the returns are on it. This will exercise an inflationary effect on skilled labour costs and lead to marked wage differentials. Extending educational opportunity can reduce this scarcity value and so contribute to a reduction in income inequalities. Improvements in education are also closely correlated with labour-productivity increases, and such increases tend to have an equalising effect on income distribution.

In the case of Taiwan, equitable access to education and health, combined with a major redistribution of land, was instrumental in reducing income inequalities after 1949. In 1940 80% of Taiwan's population were illiterate, yet by the mid-1980s illiteracy had been virtually eradicated, with nine years of compulsory schooling provided free to every child. The health status of the population has seen similarly dramatic improvements. The crude death rate is 5 per 1000, and life expectancy is 70.5 years for men and 75.5 for women. These high average human-capital levels, combined with radical land reform and the fact that labour-intensive growth was based on small firms competing for a highly skilled labour pool, had a marked effect on income distribution. In the early 1950s the Gini Coefficient of household income distribution stood at 0.558, almost identical to that of Guatemala. By 1978, at 0.289 Taiwan had the most equal income distribution outside the socialist world. This distributional shift, unprecedented in a capitalist economy, took place against a backdrop of average annual GNP growth rates exceeding 8%.[14]

While Taiwan's experience illustrates the clear benefits, in terms of equity and growth, of good-quality universal health care and education provision, increasing the supply of social provision can have very different outcomes, depending on the wider development strategy being pursued. The contrasting experiences of Brazil and South Korea again reveal the importance of education to income-distribution patterns. In the 1950s, Brazil's primary-completion rate was 60%, whereas that of South Korea, then a low-income country, was 36%. Yet today, whereas almost all South Korean children complete the primary cycle, one third of Brazilian children fail to do so. In Brazil, poor educational performance and inefficient spending combined with weak demand for labour to widen inequalities and inhibit poverty reduction. In contrast, the labour-intensive nature of Korean growth meant that rising levels of educational attainment compressed wages differentials during the 1960s. The supply of skilled labour was expanding, with the benefits of growth being shared increasingly equitably. Over the two decades up to the mid-1980s, the average income of those who had completed higher education declined from 97% above the average wage to 66% above it. In Brazil, over the same period, the earnings of those with higher education had reached 156% of the average wage. The failure to improve the quality of education and to link it to livelihood strategies was a key factor behind increasing inequality in Brazil.[15]

Just as extending access to basic services can reduce income inequalities, so neglecting social provision for the majority perpetuates and exacerbates income inequalities. Countries which under-attain in education and health for their level of GDP tend to have exceptionally high levels of poverty and inequality, just as countries which over-attain educationally relative to GDP tend to have lower poverty levels than would be expected, and relatively equitable distribution of income and assets. The correlation between income distribution and social-sector performance is especially strong when Latin America and East Asia are compared. Where the major Latin American countries have routinely under-performed in educating their populations, the East Asian countries have constantly added to their existing human-capital stock.

In Brazil and Mexico, the mean years of schooling are two fewer (five rather than seven) than would be expected for their income level.[16] Health indicators are similarly poor: Brazil, Mexico, Venezuela, and Peru all have below-average life expectancy, given their income levels, with Peru's life expectancy 'gap' at five years.[17] The levels of income inequality and income poverty in Latin America over the last three decades have remained stubbornly high, as much because of the failure to improve access and quality in social provision and so raise productivity and decrease the levels of return to scarce human capital, as because of asset distribution, which has diminished in importance as the region has become increasingly urbanised.

Social provision: not a stand-alone strategy

Notwithstanding the crucial role of social provision in promoting equitable growth, expenditure on education and health will not single-handedly lead to poverty eradication. Social provision cannot be isolated from other factors in promoting development: unless good social outcomes promote viable livelihood opportunities for the poor, social and economic development is likely to be jeopardised. With human capital, unlike land or physical capital, distributional outcomes can be improved upon simply by adding to the existing stock. As a result, investment in human capital is an attractive strategy for economists otherwise opposed to redistributive policies. But social provision is insufficient by itself as a pro-growth strategy. Social provisioning needs to be co-ordinated with other policies to promote equitable patterns of growth — labour-intensive investment incentives, land redistribution, stable prices, progressive and efficient tax systems, transparent legal process, macro-economic stability, access to credit and savings facilities, communications and transport development — if equitable economic growth is going to be achieved.

While high-quality social provisioning in East Asia was co-ordinated with a range of other redistributive measures and fed into the growth process, in countries such as Sri Lanka, Cuba, and Zimbabwe it has clearly had less success. In Sri Lanka, open unemployment rates close to 15% reflect the failure to develop a labour-intensive growth strategy. And in Cuba, the continuing dependence on a sugar monoculture, and the distortions of imported Soviet planners, whose prescriptions limited the range of market opportunities for the poor, clearly offset many of the potential economic benefits that the excellent health and education systems might otherwise have brought. In Zimbabwe a small, inefficient, and heavily subsidised manufacturing sector and grossly unequal distribution of assets have limited the returns to educational investment, with the rate of increase in new labour-market recruits far exceeding the rate of job creation.

Social provisioning also needs to be co-ordinated with a range of other redistributive strategies and institutional reforms for socially embedded inequalities to be reduced. There is widespread evidence that universal social provisioning does little by itself to reduce inequality between men and women. Even in countries where average levels of education and experience for women are higher than those for men — such as Jamaica and Ecuador — men's wage levels are still 20-30% higher than women's.[18]

And, as observed by the Black Report, a 1980 study of living standards in Britain, although the introduction of universal free health care in the late 1940s led to dramatic reductions in child and maternal mortality over a 30-year period, there was little impact on health inequalities between income groups.[19] The findings of the Black Report point to an important lesson. Reducing inequalities depends on a range of factors in addition to social provision. These include livelihood opportunities, working conditions, and less tangible development goals such as social cohesion, and political and cultural inclusion. Enhancing well-being demands that policy makers pay close attention to all these areas.

Problems with the market in social provision

How social provision for all is best achieved has been the focus of much debate over the last two decades, usually over the role of the state as provider and regulator, as against the role of the market mechanism in ensuring optimal outcomes.[20] This debate — often linked with the wider ideological dispute between state interventionism, or 'dirigisme', and market liberalism — has been especially vigorous in developing countries where market features have been extensively introduced to health and education systems. The underlying disagreement concerns whether or not health and education can (and should) in certain circumstances — especially for higher-level services — be treated like any other commodity in the marketplace, left to develop according to demand, with consumers paying a market rate for the services they use.

Market liberals point to the inefficiency and poor quality of service which characterises many state providers, and the contrasting efficiency and high quality of many commercial providers who openly compete in the market for consumers. Other service-providers, it is noted — architects, engineers, lawyers, bankers — function effectively with limited state intervention. They set their own standards through professional bodies and monitor these, knowing it is in their own interest to do so. There is no good reason why things should be any different in social provision, it is argued: the state should retreat where possible from financing and providing education and health services, and the private sector should be encouraged to take the principal, or at least an enlarged role, in social provision. Where the state does continue to operate basic 'safety net' services, efficiency gains can be made by introducing user-charges and by simulating market behaviour — through the creation of 'internal markets' and the introduction of voucher schemes.

Market demand and social need

Yet the parallels drawn by market liberals between health and education and other services are weak. There are shared features of health and education which lead to problems when the market mechanism is left to allocate resources. This helps to explain the level of state intervention in social provision in the industrialised and developing countries as something more than a simple accident of history. The role of the state as funder and provider has come about because health care and education function very differently from other perceived necessities that are purchased in the market, such as food and clothing.

Firstly, leaving social provision to the market leads to strongly unequal results, as the case of China's recent experiences, discussed below, demonstrates. The market responds only to market demand generated through purchasing power. Because ill health and poor educational attainment limit income-earning opportunities, and therefore purchasing power, those in greatest need end up being those least able to pay. And because education in particular increases earnings capacity, with attainment levels closely linked to future income,[21] leaving education provision to respond to market demand reinforces income inequalities and severely limits income-group mobility. The wealthiest households can afford the best and most education, and poor households the least. The result is that poverty is transmitted to the next generation. Though health care restores rather than — in most cases — increases our earnings capacity, the effect of leaving health provision to respond to effective demand is similar. Incomes strongly affect the capacity of individuals to stay healthy, so that poor households unable to afford medical care, or forced into distress-sales of assets, are more likely to experience falls in income as a result of illness.

Education and health care differ from most other purchases in other important ways. In the case of education, the consumer needs to purchase schooling on a regular and long-term basis in order to become educated — UNESCO estimates four years of schooling to be the standard minimum required to attain functional literacy — and this requires a predictable and regular source of income, something that poor households are usually lacking. Because education involves participation over a number of years, the opportunity costs are also high, especially for poor households. As children grow older, these opportunity costs usually continue to rise, as children consume more and their income-earning opportunities increase. While the opportunity costs of much health care are low, since purchases are typically infrequent and brief, costs are highly unpredictable and often large. Because the poor are often excluded from credit markets, individuals may have to forgo treatment, or are forced into distress-sales of land, cattle, and other income-generating assets in order to finance purchases. Either way, the equity costs are substantial.

Secondly, market failure is risked where health and education provision is left to respond to market demand, because of shared and particular characteristics.

■ There are considerable social as well as private returns to human-capital investment. Some of the beneficial 'spillover' effects of education have already been described. In health, curing a person of a communicable disease benefits not only the individual, but also those people who would have otherwise have contracted it. Though a child benefits significantly in terms of health and nutrition from having an educated mother, independently of income, few benefits are captured by the parents who pay for their daughter's education, especially where she is married into another household. Leaving education or health provision to the household has especially damaging effects on gender equity. The result of leaving the market to respond to market demand in social provision tends to be under-consumption, because the costs and benefits of an investment are calculated by most people only in terms of their own interests.

■ In health and education services there are extreme asymmetries of information between the consumer and the provider. This demands a high level of trust, especially since the costs of making a bad purchase in the social sectors are usually high, and sometimes fatal. Because health staff are both the advisers on the type of service needed *and* the providers, there is almost limitless scope for commercial health-care providers to mislead patients, as demonstrated by revelations about a for-profit American provider, Columbia/HCA. Widespread abuses in Columbia's hospitals included giving patients expensive unnecessary treatments, overcharging patients for treatments they did need, and referring patients to 'affiliated' specialists when it was not in their best interests.[22]

■ Partly because of the time-lag between making a purchase and the returns to that purchase, consumers are often unaware of the private returns to human-capital investment, and they fail to act in rational ways that maximise utility. Hence people tend not to commit resources to preventative treatments, such as immunisations, whose effect is felt only in the longer term. For example, in Britain, the introduction of charges for dental check-ups led to a sharp reduction in the number of people, especially from lower-income groups, regularly visiting dentists.[23] The short-term priorities of most individual consumers carry wider long-term social and economic costs.

■ The usual set of consumer sanctions are not straightforwardly applicable in social provision. As the economist Albert Hirschman has noted, commercial enterprises in a market economy usually find out about their failings — and respond to them — when consumers stop buying a firm's product, and start instead to buy from a competitor. This is called the 'option of exit'.[24] But in health and education, the option of exit is usually extremely limited. It is not easy to withdraw from a course of medical treatment that is on-going; in education, where frequent disruption of a child's education can damage learning, the option of exit is even more constrained.

■ There are other market failures. Local monopolies in health and education are often unavoidable. It is questionable how much freedom of choice parents can really have — especially in rural areas – in selecting a school for their children. And implementing productivity increases frequently leads to a reduction of standards, potentially exposing patients to unacceptable risk, or limiting a child's learning.

■ In education especially, the issue of agency creates problems where provision is marketised: the consumers are not usually meeting the costs themselves. This also leads to particular difficulties with voucher schemes for education, currently endorsed by the World Bank. Because children are the consumers, one must suppose that parents who are entrusted with the decision over where they spend the vouchers have the best interests of the child at heart, as well as a real choice of schooling for their child, and the education and knowledge required to make an informed decision about their child's life-opportunities. Often, these suppositions are not justified.

■ The consumption of some forms of education and health provision cannot be easily restricted and therefore sold to an individual consumer. This has been described as the 'tragedy of the commons': if the benefits of an intervention are available to 'free riders' who have contributed nothing, it is unlikely to go ahead without public support.[25] Examples are a pest-control programme, or a public-education broadcast, which are unlikely to be financed privately.

More generally, despite the high social and private returns, there is limited market demand for mass immunisation, or mass literacy, in developing countries. Because of capital and recurrent costs both in health and education services, and the scale economies and information-gathering capacity needed to implement mass treatments or deliver a good quality of education, the market response to both market demand and social need is typically weak. The creation of welfare states in Western Europe after 1945, and the post-independence expansion in public health and education services in developing countries, were a recognition of the limits to what the market might be expected to do in response both to effective and social demand. In developing countries especially, the state remains the most effective, and often the *only* agent capable of mobilising the sort of resources needed to introduce clean water, or literacy, to entire populations. It is also usually the only agent with the institutional capacity to protect provision once it has been introduced.

Finally, if access to learning and a reasonable standard of health are regarded as basic human rights — as laid out in Articles 25 and 26 of the Universal Declaration of Human Rights — then leaving access to chance in the marketplace is unacceptable. Article 26 specifies that 'Education shall be free, at least in the elementary and fundamental stages'. At the very least, we should be wary of introducing charges for a service that we believe everybody ought to use.

Market features and access for the poor

Clearly, health and education services are not selling simply commodities, as some of the more dogmatic proponents of free markets have argued. Leaving social provision to respond simply to effective demand is fundamentally different from allowing the market in foreign holidays or televisions to respond to effective demand, because no other market-purchases affect our life opportunities in the way that our acquisition of education and health care does. Although the World Bank has not taken such an extreme position, too often it has endorsed the hasty introduction of market features into social provisioning for poor communities, resulting in high social costs. While universal access can be achieved by a number of policy mixes, the role of the state in mobilising public finance and protecting basic services is essential.

While in some instances paying the private sector to provide basic services may be more effective than setting up a state facility, without tight regulation and high levels of purchasing power the equity costs are likely to be high. Although in South Korea, where almost 90 per cent of all health facilities are privately owned, the compulsory National Health Insurance system has been largely successful in protecting access for the poor and continuing to improve the health status of the Korean population,[26] this system would not be replicable in a poor developing country. In most developing countries, economies are too small and demand is too thin for effective health and education markets to exist.

Even where purchasing power is high, without tight regulation the effects of commercial provision are likely to be profoundly uneven. In the USA, minimal public provision, combined with weak health regulation, has created a situation where 15% of Americans go through life without any form of health insurance. The health profile of lower-income groups is correspondingly poor, and the system notoriously inefficient. Americans currently spend 15% of GDP a year, or an astonishing one trillion dollars, on direct and indirect providers of health care, a sum three times larger than the whole of sub-Saharan Africa's economic output. Not only is per capita health spending in the USA two to three times greater than health expenditure in other industrialised countries, but the richest country in the world performs worse in health indicators such as infant mortality than Cuba and Slovenia.[27]

Box 2.1 The costs of marketising health care: the case of China

China's experiences in health provision over the last five decades illustrate both the capacity of poor countries to achieve rapid human development with modest resources, and the equity costs and poverty impact of marketising social provision. China's health system developed over a 30-year period after the revolution as a cost-effective response to crushing rural poverty on a vast scale, and provided a strong basis for subsequent rapid economic growth. China was one of only 12 countries which between 1960 and 1980 moved from low to medium human development. Despite inflexibilities, the 'iron rice bowl' system ensured very equitable access to basic services, and there was not a wide disparity in health outcomes between rural and urban areas. Communes and users funded the rural health stations, while health workers were paid as members of the commune, creating a user-driven pressure for accountability and efficiency.

After 1978, the commune system began to be dismantled as part of the economic liberalisation programme, and there was wholesale change in health funding and provisioning. In place of the communes, household production was restored, and as a result, the health system lost its financial base in rural areas. By the early 1990s only 10% of the rural population had access to a co-operative health facility. The government cut spending as the system of barefoot doctors was abolished, and user-charges became a growing component of rural health-scheme incomes. Whereas out-of-pocket payments accounted for one fifth of health spending in 1978, they now account for close to half. Private health care was legalised, and boomed in urban areas, where liberalisation soon raised average incomes. This change in funding patterns reflects wholesale structural change in the system: co-ordination between curative and preventative services has been reduced, while a quasi-commercial 'fiscal responsibility system' has been introduced, allowing health facilities to use surplus revenue for employee pay rises and reinvestment.

The reforms have had three major effects: first, introducing elements of a competitive labour market exacerbated regional inequalities. Isolated interior provinces such as Yunnan, which has a poverty rate more than three times the national average, have largely missed out on recent economic growth. Average purchasing power remains extremely low in rural areas, and labour-market opportunities are few. As a result, health personnel were drawn into the cities, where medicine can be a lucrative trade. What started as a trickle of skilled labour from rural to urban areas is now an exodus, as poor areas with limited tax bases find themselves unable to compete on salary levels. Today, 15 per cent of China's population, almost entirely urban, utilise 44% of China's health resources.

Second, the financial impact of health-care changes in provinces such as Yunnan has been profound. Health services that were previously free of charge have been phased out, along with income transfers such as subsidies, food parcels and workplace meals. According to the Ministry of Health, rural households were spending an average of 9% of household income on health care by 1993, with the average charge for in-patient treatment representing 60% of net income. In Yuhan county, Zhejiang, close to half of the households below the poverty line reported health costs as the principal factor forcing them into poverty.

Third, the reforms precipitated a decline in welfare indicators, with especially adverse effects on women and girls. Although from 1978 to 1984, a period of unusually good harvests, dramatic reductions in income-poverty took place in the countryside as well as in urban areas, there was no commensurate improvement in welfare indicators. In fact, the opposite happened, with a dramatic rise in infant mortality from 37.2 to 50.1 deaths per thousand live births over this six-year period.[28]

The reasons for this deterioration, which has not yet been fully reversed, are complex. The erosion of access to health facilities as a result of increased direct and opportunity costs was a major reason, but a contributory factor is believed to be the changes in the rural division of labour. The dismantling of commune agriculture saw a return to a traditional gendered division of labour in many rural households. The loss of the status that had been conferred on women by their roles in the commune, and the perceived lower economic returns to women's labour once they were returned to the household were likely factors in the marked increase in female infant mortality rates in the early 1980s, with widespread anecdotal reports of increases in infanticide of girls.[29] The 15% rise in child malnutrition between 1987 and 1994 (which has coincided with the emergence of child obesity as a serious health problem) similarly appears to reflect in part the prioritisation of boys' nutritional needs in poor households.

Clearly, the replacement of the iron rice bowl with the competitive rigours of the market has led to a severe erosion in access to social provision, and a deepening of poverty for vulnerable social groups — poor farmers, unskilled women, labour migrants — whom growth has by-passed. Post-reform failures in the health-care system are the result not only of introducing into impoverished communities a system based on the ability to pay, but also of introducing gender-blind policies into a society where there are entrenched biases against women and girls. Whatever the allocative inefficiencies of the pre-reform health system, it generally succeeded in protecting the basic needs of China's population; the record of the market is much less convincing. The case of China demonstrates the costs of introducing market features to social-service systems in a poor country. Marked inequalities in health status across regions, sexes, and income groups have been the result, with long-term implications for social stability, poverty reduction, and growth.

Financing social provision in developing countries

Despite the negative experiences of countries such as China which have introduced market features into social provision (see Box 2.1), since the mid-1980s governments have widely experimented with market features in social provision in an attempt to bring efficiency gains to bloated health and education systems. The World Bank has been one of the most influential advocates of market features in health and education, and has variously promoted user-charges and voucher schemes in an attempt to improve the returns on social investment. Particularly in sub-Saharan

Africa, the World Bank played an instrumental role in the marketisation of social provision through its policy analysis on education and health-care financing during the 1980s. This work provided an influential rationale for the introduction of charges, and competition between 'service providers' as a way of improving both the quality and efficiency of education and health care.

Economists in favour of market-based social provision justify their theories by forwarding three distinct arguments. First, it is claimed that in the poorest countries governments cannot afford universal social provision. The revenue pool is small, the full range of traditional revenue instruments is already being used, and new sources of finance must be found. It is argued that charging fees for public services, and encouraging private-sector growth, would release more resources and relieve some of the fiscal pressures on government. Second, they cite the misallocation of resources in many developing counties' health and education systems, which all too often reflects the short-term political priorities of governments (building state-of-the-art hospitals and universities which are used predominantly by influential urban constituencies), rather than the basic needs of the poor majority. But with the added resources generated through fees, it is argued that government would be able to direct resources to those areas of provisioning where need and social returns were greatest (among the poor). Third, advocates of a marketised system cite the low quality and internal inefficiency of public providers. With schools competing for students, and clinics — or individual health staff — competing for patients, teachers and health workers would be given a direct stake in their organisation. The envisaged result would be the eradication of internal inefficiencies.

None of these arguments in fact makes a case for an increasing market role in social provision. Rather, they are a set of observations about state failure. This position reflects a deep pessimism about the ability of developing-country governments to deliver improvements in the standard of living to their populations: since corrupt and ineffectual government is the malaise, it is reasoned, it cannot be a part of the cure. That many developing-country health-care and education systems fail to deliver adequate social provisioning is not in dispute. However, several points need to be made in response to the position of the market proponents. Firstly, the question of affordability is debatable. Because both health and education systems are highly labour-intensive, with most recurrent costs accounted for by staff salaries, primary education and health care are usually cheap to provide. A heterogeneous group of low-income countries — China, Vietnam, Sri Lanka, Zimbabwe — have succeeded in near-universal health and education provision, and dramatic improvements in welfare indicators, through state provision. Despite the retreat from universal public health and education provision in some of these countries (see above), they demonstrate that low income need not be a bar to relatively efficient and equitable public provision, and that 'state failure' is far from universal. Even the worst performers in education and health, in the poorest countries, have made considerable improvements in literacy, morbidity, and mortality rates over the last three decades, most of these advances a result of state intervention.

Secondly, where cost-recovery has been introduced for health care and education, few extra resources have in fact been mobilised. Net revenues have been far lower than gross revenues, because collection costs are typically high.[30] All too often, means-testing to guarantee a safety net proves impractical, especially in African countries where average purchasing power is very low and means-testing has spawned new bureaucracies, offsetting many of the financial gains made from the introduction of cost-recovery.

Moreover, the presumption that any extra revenues will go directly into improving health and education services for the poor — as opposed to serving as a pretext for budget cuts — is not based on the experience of countries such as Zambia, Zimbabwe, and Tanzania. In these countries, Oxfam's partners work with some of the poorest communities, for whom the results of cost-recovery — introduced during IMF and World Bank adjustment programmes — have been disastrous. The community retention of fees envisaged by the World Bank simply did not happen, while safety-net systems for the poorest households were typically introduced *after* cost-recovery had been introduced. In one Zambian hospital, attendance fell by 50% over the five years after the introduction of user fees, and a 1995 report came to the unequivocal conclusion that 'user fees have continued to place the formal health system beyond the reach of the poor'.[31] In Zimbabwe, the number of women *not* registering for neo-natal care in the two years afters the introduction of user fees increased by 30%. In the 1990 to 1992 period, real expenditure on health fell by almost a quarter. In these two years, the number of Zimbabwean women dying during pregnancy and childbirth rose from 190 for every 100,000 cases to 265 for every 100,000 cases.[32]

A further argument put forward in favour of cost-recovery is that introducing user-charges for services where there is substantial under-provision is an effective way of extending access. Despite claims by the

World Bank that demand for health care in particular is insensitive to price, and that resultant improvements in the quality and efficiency of service lead to improved equity and access, the evidence is that the introduction of user-charges in health care and primary schools tends to lead to a deterioration in access and falling enrolments. The equity costs of user-charges are considerable, since it is the poorest households who typically withdraw their children (usually girls before boys) from school, and who go without essential health services. Even where there is no evidence of reduced use of services, and poor households choose to pay for services, willingness to pay needs to be distinguished from ability to pay. Households — or certain household members — may nonetheless be reducing their consumption of other essentials, such as food, which can affect their long-term productivity. None of this ought to be surprising. After all, where the opposite has happened, and user-charges have been reduced or abolished, there is evidence of marked improvements in access and equity. This happened in Malawi, where user-charges for primary education were abolished in 1994. The enrolment response was dramatic. During the first year of free primary education, enrolment rose by 58%.[33] Least supportable of all is the frequently stated claim, made by many supporters of user-charges, that falls in service consumption after charges have been introduced denote efficiency gains among service providers. This seems hard to support, unless it is argued that in developing countries there is widespread and frivolous over-consumption of free health-care and education systems.

In conclusion, the experiments with marketisation of social provision — especially at the primary level and in developing countries with low average purchasing power — suggest that both equity and access will suffer, with serious long-term consequences for growth and poverty. While in some exceptional circumstances, cost recovery may be necessary to maintain basic services, if only as an interim measure, the tight regulation and administrative transparency needed to protect access for the poor contrast with the relatively weak managerial capacities of social services in most developing countries. The experiences of sub-Saharan Africa demonstrate that, however inefficient state providers may be, marketising provision is no panacea. While there is often a case for the introduction of means-tested user-charges for sophisticated curative health care, and for fees and loans for upper-secondary and tertiary education, not least where this releases resources for improved basic provision, even the poorest countries must treat universal, free, basic health care and education as the minimum standard. Generally, aiming for a more equitable and efficient allocation of existing social expenditure will achieve far more than will any moves towards providing basic services according to the user's ability to pay. Even in the most narrowly economic terms, introducing market features to health and education systems leads to results which are far from efficient.

Social provision: access, quality, and equity

Every day, across the developing world, tens of millions of children are denied the opportunity to learn, decades after education came to be accepted as a universal right. Each day thousands of people, mostly children, die prematurely from easily preventable diseases. The underlying causes of these human tragedies are complex. Yet the widespread failure on the part of states to provide effective public services to people living in poverty is a key factor in the growing disparities in health status and educational attainment, both between the North and the South and within countries.

Often, the headline figures obscure as much as they reveal about the true dimensions of the human-development deficit in the world's poorest regions. Take the case of education. Behind the enrolment figures lie millions of lost opportunities to learn, cut short by early entry into labour markets. While most children in developing countries now enrol in a school, more than a quarter of them will fail to complete even five years of formal education. Most of those who do drop out do so in the first or second year of schooling. The children who drop out earliest, and in the largest numbers, are girls.[34] The majority of them leave without even basic literacy and numeracy skills, reinforcing a cycle of poverty, lack of opportunity, and low productivity. For those children who do remain in school, the quality of teaching is often poor, the school day and year are short, and little is learned. More often than not, schools in developing countries are grossly under-resourced, teachers themselves have only the most basic primary education, and staff absenteeism and student non-attendance are widespread.

Given the crucial role of education in breaking inter-generational poverty links, reducing income and social inequalities, and contributing to wealth creation, the current provision of education in the South can properly be described as being in crisis. Although significant advances were made in extending educational opportunity by the post-independence countries of Africa and Asia, progress since 1980 has slowed, and in some instances been reversed. As Table 2.3 illustrates, in sub-Saharan Africa there have been absolute and proportionate rises in the number of children out of school in recent years, while the South Asian countries continue to underperform abysmally — particularly in educating girls. Educational underperformance stands as a major obstacle to economic growth and poverty reduction in these two regions. In Latin America and East Asia, while enrolment figures are better, the quality and length of compulsory education are extremely uneven, and secondary education remains the privilege largely of urban upper-income groups. Schooling for all, the target set for the year 2000 at the Jomtien Conference in Thailand, will remain a distant prospect well into the new millennium without concerted action from governments in the South, and supportive policies from aid donors in the North.[35] The message is a stark one: without on-going improvements in the quality of and access to education, growth and equity will continue to suffer.

In many cases, the education crisis reflects under-supply. For millions of people living in poverty, schooling is simply unavailable. For a range of reasons, in many developing countries public education has not expanded at the same rate of increase as the expansion in demand. The countries that have had least success in meeting needs have a number of shared characteristics: high levels of poverty and income inequality, large rural populations, rapid population growth, large external debts, and recent economic records ranging from the disappointing to the disastrous. The final characteristic — that of slow growth or no growth — has also been instrumental in reducing demand for social services, as will be shown in the next section.

Table 2.3 Children out of school: some regional disparities
(Source: UNESCO 1995)

Country/region	1960	1980	1990	2000
sub-Saharan Africa				
millions	25	26	41	59
%	75%	43%	50%	51%
Latin America				
millions	15	9	8	7
%	43%	18%	13%	11%
East Asia				
millions	67	55	26	27
%	47%	25%	13%	12%

As has already been argued, inequalities of income and assets are closely linked to under-enrolment, reflecting education budgets distorted in favour of powerful, mostly urban, constituencies. In rural areas, the average, or unit, cost of education is usually higher than in urban areas. Schools are smaller, teachers often are paid more highly, in order to compensate for the higher costs of living, and materials have to be transported farther. This means that for developing countries with predominantly rural populations, extending education and health provision is both more expensive than for more urbanised countries, and involves particular logistical challenges. This is especially the case where rural regions are sparsely populated, as in much of Latin America and Africa. Distances to and from schools and health facilities have been shown to be major factors in educational enrolment rates and the frequency of visits to clinics.[36]

Rapid population growth presents further difficulties to governments committed to universal social provision, particularly in education, where provision is directed primarily at the 5–15 age group. This is because the larger the school-age population as a proportion of the total, the larger the proportion of GNP needed to achieve universal education. In the developing countries, particularly those in sub-Saharan Africa, the population profile is that of a 'pyramid', with the under-15 age group accounting for upwards of one third of the population, and often as much as one half. Whereas in the industrial countries children of primary-school age account for 5-8% of the population, and in China for 12%, in sub-Saharan Africa and South Asia 15–20% of the population is typically of primary-school age.[37] The typical dependency ratio of poor countries (the proportion of the working-age population, conventionally defined as 15–64, as a proportion of the total population) means that universal education places heavy demands on the economically active population, who must pay taxes to finance education, as well as feed and clothe their children. The burden of education spending as a proportion of GNP in Africa rose from 5.3% of GNP in 1980 to 6.1% in 1994, although declining per capita expenditure has meant that per capita absolute expenditures have continued to fall.[38]

In a country with a rapidly growing population such as Kenya, the demands that schooling for all makes of the working-age group are extreme. The 15–64 age group accounts for only 14 million people out of a population of 27 million. Meanwhile primary enrolment has fallen by 15% since 1980, despite an actual rise in the proportion of GNP being spent on education.[39] With most poor countries having population growth rates of between 2.5% and 3.5% every year, new schools must be built, and teachers recruited and trained (and therefore the secondary and tertiary sectors expanded), all at a rapid pace. In the context of slow or negative per capita growth, the norm for the last 15 years in much of sub-Saharan Africa and Latin America, a weak revenue-raising capacity, and rising debt-service payments,[40] maintaining educational standards while at the same extending access is an enormous challenge, requiring wholehearted commitment from the state. All too often, this has not been forthcoming.

Given the huge scale of unmet demand for educational services across the South — matched by a similar unmet demand for health care – it is necessary to ask who can possibly meet it. The marketisation of provision has not been the panacea that some had believed it would be. Where market features have been introduced into health and education provision, and supply left to respond to effective demand, equity and access have generally suffered. In short, market failure is not the cure for state failure. Instead, the state's role in social provision needs to be strengthened if the millions of people currently denied access to education and health care are to see a change in their standard of living. Although the circumstances under which many of the poorest countries struggle to supply adequate health care and education are difficult, the status quo is neither tolerable nor inevitable. In fact, many of the worst performers in primary enrolment and basic health care have protected expenditures which favour the wealthy and urban population, with secondary and tertiary enrolment rising as primary enrolment has fallen (see Table 2.4). Though every society needs skilled professionals, not least in the health and education sectors, a balance needs to be struck in the poorest countries between funding basic services, where social returns are highest, and higher education and sophisticated curative health care,

Table 2.4: Primary and secondary gross enrolments in Africa (%)

(Source: African Development Bank, African Development Report 1997)

Country	PRIMARY		SECONDARY	
	1980	1993	1980	1993
Côte d'Ivoire	79	69	19	25
Ethiopia	35	23	9	11
Morocco	83	73	26	35
Nigeria	104	93	19	29

where social returns are lowest. It may be necessary for governments to use private finance to fund those services currently used overwhelmingly by upper-income groups, redirecting scarce finances to meeting basic needs.

Governments with a poor track record in social provision must prioritise basic services and meet their commitments to poverty eradication. A misallocation of resources, under-investment, and a shrinking revenue base in many developing-country economies where per capita incomes are stagnant or falling all create under-supply. Yet even the poorest governments are able to provide basic social-service provision. The ingredient most often in short supply is not money, but political will.

Social expenditure and social outcomes

As demonstrated by the experience of Kerala, even the poorest governments can achieve dramatic results in the fields of health and education. Meanwhile, many high-spending middle-income countries have singularly failed to translate growth into poverty reduction. Because the social rates of return on basic human-capital investment are extremely high, a human-development strategy is both affordable and desirable for the poorest countries. Sri Lanka is one example of a low-income country bringing about, at low costs, welfare outcomes at the primary level which closely resemble those of the industrialised countries. Only once a society's disease profile comes to resemble that of the industrialised countries — one dominated by chronic conditions — are there significantly diminished returns on further investment in health care. The data from low-income countries which have prioritised improved health outcomes suggest that life expectancy of 70 years or over, and infant mortality rates of around 30 deaths per thousand live births are attainable at a low cost.

As Table 2.5 clearly shows, in health the relationship between expenditure and outcome, and between numbers of medical staff and outcomes, is a weak one. Most notable is the spectacular under-achievement of Brazil, which spends almost 15 times per person what is spent in China and yet has worse health outcomes. In Brazil's major cities, expertise and standards in the best private health-care facilities are comparable to those available in London or New York. Yet Brazil manages to combine First World services for the few with barely existent services for the majority, with the result that in some parts of the country social indicators compare with those for the poorest sub-Saharan African

Table 2.5: Social expenditure: quality, not quantity, matters

(Source: World Bank, *World Development Indicators 1997; note that per capita health expenditure includes public and private spending)*

Country	Per capita health expenditure 1995 US$	Child mortality per 1000 births 1995	Life exp. (years) 1995	People per physician 1993
China	22	43	69	1,063
India	12	95	62	2,459
Brazil	320	57	67	844
Costa Rica	260	16	77	1,133
Vietnam	14	49	68	2,279
Philippines	26	53	66	8,273
Sri Lanka	14	19	72	6,843
Indonesia	15	75	64	7,028

countries. Though extreme by Latin American standards, the case of Brazil is not untypical: and across the region the number of people not covered by formal health care is double what it should be, relative to income and expenditure. In Peru, Bolivia, Guatemala, Ecuador, Honduras, Haiti, El Salvador, and Paraguay, more than 40 per cent of the population are without access to health facilities.[41] Yet there is no necessary reason why this should be the case. Recent successes in extending and improving health-care provision in the Brazilian state of Ceara show how, even in impoverished and politically corrupt environments such as north-east Brazil, dramatic advances in human welfare with small budgets are possible (see Box 2.2).

Again, as the contrasting health indicators in Vietnam and India suggest, expenditure has a limited impact on health outcomes, and the way in which spending is distributed is equally important. Because Vietnam's health-care system, modelled on China's pre-reform set-up of barefoot doctors and primary preventative health care, prioritised basic treatments for the poor, dramatic improvements in welfare indicators took place in only 15 years. In India, almost identical per capita health expenditure has been disproportionately concentrated in sophisticated tertiary care for an urban minority, while health needs in rural areas have suffered persistent neglect. The result is that in India a child is twice as likely to die before the age of 5 as a child in Vietnam, while life expectancy in India is six years shorter.

Box 2.2   Health and participation in Brazil: a success story

In the north-eastern Brazilian state of Ceara, a health project jointly funded by municipal and state government, based on participatory principles, has achieved dramatic results in infant mortality and morbidity rates, suggesting that there is much that can be done to improve social provision by involving local communities, even in countries like Brazil that are more commonly associated with gross inequalities and rent-seeking behaviour in public life.[42] Ceara is one of the poorest states in Brazil, notorious for its corrupt administration and the routine use of public funds for political patronage. It covers an area similar in size to Uruguay, and is home to six and a half million people, one third of whom live in absolute poverty, unable to meet even their most basic food needs. In 1987, when the Programa de Agentes de Saude (PAS) was initiated, the infant mortality rate stood at 102 per 1,000 live births, and only a quarter of all children had been vaccinated for measles and polio. Only 30% of Ceara's counties had any formal health service, and most people in Ceara depended principally upon traditional medicines. In many counties the only medical provision was from the mayor's office, where a store of medicines and an ambulance were kept for use by family and friends. Yet by 1993 infant mortality had been almost halved to 65 cases per thousand live births; vaccination rates for polio and measles had tripled and covered three quarters of all children; almost all 178 counties had active nurses; and 850,000 families were being visited in their homes every month by a health agent — 65% of the state population over the year – to be given advice on prenatal care, breast-feeding and growth-monitoring, and vaccinations and oral rehydration treatment.

A combination of community mobilisation, a transparent system of labour hiring, based on merit, and joint funding by municipal and state government, preventing overall political control of the programme, contributed to the success of the Programme. PAS was the result of an emergency employment programme in 1987 in response to a drought in Ceara. It was funded largely through collecting taxes already on the books and 'laying off' an army of phantom workers. Costs were split between state and municipal government, giving local mayors some incentive to co-operate in a programme they feared would reduce their powers of patronage, and yet limited their scope for clientelistic behaviour. Programme costs were low: $2 per capita per year, or an annual budget of $7–8m, and 80 per cent of these costs were wages. 7,300 unskilled local health agents were recruited, along with 235 nurses who played a supervisory role. Health agents were paid the minimum wage of $60 a month, a good wage for public-sector employees in Ceara, while the supervisors were paid $300 a month, more than they would earn even in an urban hospital. State government retained firm control over the procedure for hiring and firing health agents, and contracts were temporary, with no fringe benefits. In a culture where public-sector jobs are widely regarded as sinecures for life, the use of temporary contracts and generous remuneration were important incentives for good performance. Perhaps most important was the meritocratic hiring process, involving heavily publicised vacancies and interviews which conferred status on the health agents as people who deserved their posts. After recruitment, intensive training for health agents, on-going publicity about PAS, and prizes for counties with the best performance instilled a sense of loyalty and commitment rare among public-sector employees in Brazil.

Ceara's poor live mainly in rural areas, where government is associated with powerful land-owning interests, and people are traditionally wary of arbitrary official interventions. Outsiders were viewed with suspicion, and not generally welcomed over the threshold of family homes. There was limited familiarity with modern medicines, and in many communities traditional healers commanded considerable respect. In such a context, making effective health interventions was inevitably going to be a difficult task, and depended on the trust and involvement of local people. Persuading mothers that breast milk was not 'sour', that washing hands with soap before food preparation helped their children's health, and that refuse should not be disposed of in the street required gaining the trust of adults and challenging deeply ingrained assumptions. In recognition of this challenge, a number of policies were adopted which helped to gain access to mothers and children.

- Health-agent posts were given mainly to women, who had often had children of their own, had a better understanding of child-rearing than men, and were more likely to enjoy the trust of the mothers they were visiting.

- Health agents were required to live locally, in areas they knew and where they were known. There was a strong sense of pride among many communities that one of their number had been chosen for the post of agent.

- The scope for corrupt, rent-seeking behaviour and preferential treatment for family and friends was generally controlled by on-going publicity on radio, stressing the role of the health agents and the channels available for complaint in cases of corruption or shirking. Health agents were required to visit a set number of households every day.

- Communities were consistently reminded that the health projects were theirs, and that high infant mortality was a source of shame for the community. Expectations were high, and the community as a whole became motivated by the sense of mission with which projects were undertaken, especially during cholera epidemics.

- Interviewees not selected for the post of health agent were encouraged to report malpractice. While there was clear scope for abuse, interviewees who failed to get the jobs were told that the act of applying had itself qualified them as 'community leaders', and this gave them a feeling of continued involvement in PAS. Failed interviewees were found to be regularly reporting the good work of health agents to supervisory nurses, as well as examples of bad practice.

- Health agents used basic curative treatments, such as oral rehydration, where the effects are dramatic and almost immediate, to win the trust of mothers. This opened the door to the more difficult task of altering domestic behaviour.

PAS proved to be highly successful, without being a straightforward case of decentralising power to local government. Indeed, in Ceara there are good reasons to suppose that, had this been done, the programme would have been exploited by local mayors and turned into one more tool of patronage. 'User-driven' accountability was highly effective, both in maintaining a high level of commitment among health agents and in drawing communities into the programme and giving them a stake in it. The case of PAS shows the scope that exists, even in the poorest and most politically hostile environments, to mobilise communities and improve government through accessible social provision.

Distribution is the key

There is obviously some connection between aggregate spending levels and social outcomes — India under-spends as well as mis-spends on health and education — especially when comparing the wealthiest industrialised nations and the least developed countries. Yet the distribution of existing resources is usually the principal determinant of health and education outcomes in developing countries. Countries that prioritise basic services, set targets, and protect budgets achieve equitable outcomes which are growth-generating. Countries where resource allocation reflects short-term political objectives, rather than the needs of the poor, tend to underperform in terms of welfare outcomes, with long-term negative implications for growth and equity. In short, distribution is the key. Budgetary constraints are rarely the principal brake on the expansion and improvement of social provision. Existing social-sector budgets tend to be misallocated in three main ways.

■ *Weak and ineffective administrative structures* carry high opportunity costs for the poor. Ineffective bureaucracies often arise because staff are poorly paid and irregularly paid, and there are few effective incentives for good performance. In many developing countries, administrative systems are also highly centralised, delaying decision making and de-motivating staff. Corruption often arises as a result of these internal efficiencies, eroding the ethos of public service. In the case of Venezuela, 20% of central government expenditure is allocated to education, yet outcomes are poor. One tenth of children never even enrol at a school, and more than one fifth of children fail to reach the fifth grade of school. Secondary-school enrolment, meanwhile, is only 35%. The explanation for this is found in the state's payroll. Venezuela's oil revenues have long sustained a huge payroll of phantom public officials who either do not exist or who never turn up for work, 'jobs' being commonly used as a tool of political patronage. The result is that the education ministry employs 340,000 people, more than Mexico's education ministry, and in a country with only one fifth of Mexico's population.[43]

■ *Biased spending on politically powerful upper-income groups.* Money is often invested in prestige projects, such as universities and hospitals, which benefit a minority, at the cost of adequate basic provision for the poor. In Colombia, the children of the wealthiest quintile benefit from *three times* as much public-education expenditure as those of the poorest quintile, despite the widespread use of private education among the wealthiest Colombians.[44] Tertiary education in Venezuela accounts for almost double the expenditure of primary and secondary education combined, while in Zambia over half of the health budget is spent on a central teaching hospital in Lusaka, in the context of a 50 per cent fall in health spending over the 1990–1994 period.

■ *Failure to develop rural social strategies.* Post-independence India has successfully created a technocratic, professional elite through its education system, and high-quality health services for a minority. But it has spectacularly failed to address rural poverty. One problem is under-spending on primary education and health care. But another problem, often overlooked, is that operating a competitive labour market in health and education in a country like India leads to a scarcity of teachers and doctors in rural areas. Wage opportunities and the standard of living in the villages of Uttar Pradesh and Orissa are unlikely to attract skilled professionals in a competitive labour market. And it is in rural areas that poverty is deepest and most prevalent. Without empowering social changes, few productive alternatives are open to Indian villagers, and the failure to develop a rural human-development strategy is a major factor behind grinding rural poverty. In rural Uttar Pradesh, with a population of over 100 million, only 10% of villages have health facilities, and 70% of girls are never enrolled in a school.[45] In rural Brazil, neglect of rural development has similarly led to endemic poverty. Only 4% of people in rural Brazil have access to sanitation facilities, and ten million people are without clean water, while health-service coverage is lower and infant mortality higher than in Indonesia.[46]

Misallocation of social-sector budgets is frequently compounded by distorted overall spending patterns. This is seen at its most extreme in non-productive expenditures such as the military. In 1997 Peru purchased 12 second-hand MIG-29 jets from Belarus — which may never fly, due to a Russian boycott on parts — at a cost of $350m over and above the allocated military budget.[47] Prioritising combat aircraft over rural development in a country where more than 40 per cent of people live below the poverty line carries clear opportunity costs for people living in poverty. In Nigeria, one in five children fails to reach the age of five — a statistic almost unchanged from 1960 — yet the government in 1995 spent $1.25bn on its armed forces. In 1994, 18 Vickers Mark-3 tanks were delivered as part of a $150m deal struck in 1990, equivalent to roughly half the annual health budget.[48]

Military overspending is at its most extreme in South Asia, where it has led to the most perverse outcomes. The opportunity costs for the poor, in a region with vast unmet needs, are correspondingly high. In India three million children under the age of five die every year from easily preventable conditions, and there are as many illiterate Indians as there are North Americans. Yet the military budget is almost four times the size of the central government's combined health and education budgets.[49] While not all military expenditure is discretionary, profligacy on this scale explodes the myth that universal social provision is an unaffordable luxury for developing countries.

Subsidisation of loss-making and often highly capital-intensive state enterprises is another area from which many governments could reallocate public spending. In Uganda, state subsidies to loss-making parastatals totalled $270 million in 1995, a sum four times larger than that year's education budget. The Ugandan government is now beginning to address the problem of under-provision of education, and setting ambitious targets for increases in enrolment and expenditure (see Box 2.3).

Efficiency measures

As well as improving the distribution of public expenditure, both within existing health and education budgets and in overall budget allocation, welfare outcomes can often be improved upon through efficiency measures. Many health interventions, such as immunisations and public-education campaigns, do not require expensively trained medical staff to be carried out successfully. The barefoot-doctor system in China was an example of large-scale welfare advances being achieved at a low cost by using semi-skilled, low-cost medical staff, operating as a highly mobile health-care presence in rural areas. In Nicaragua, similar health strategies were adopted under the Sandinista government, again leading to notable successes, including a halving of what had been the highest infant mortality rate in Central America. In education, efficiency measures are less obvious, but an example would be the use of double-session teaching, morning and afternoon, to make maximum use of classrooms. In Zimbabwe, double-session teaching was central to the huge expansion in education provision that took place after 1980, reducing the capital costs of new school facilities.[50]

However, efficiency gains are often losses in terms of equity and quality, and care needs to be taken in the implementation of policies designed to reduce unit costs. In sub-Saharan Africa in particular, where recession and adjustment have squeezed budgets, measures adopted in an effort to increase the cost-effectiveness of public education have often run into problems. Class sizes have been increased, curricula rationalised, the pre-university school cycle reduced, and administrative staff laid off, but quality has suffered. Devolving financial responsibility to parents and communities for teachers, buildings, or basic materials has also been widely attempted. Unsurprisingly, educational quality has come to reflect income. The poorest communities, most in need of quality education as a route out of poverty, are left with a second-class service.

Box 2.3 Lessons from Uganda

Improving access to social provision with only limited resources is a challenge facing many Least Developed Country governments that are committed to extending health and educational provision to currently excluded groups. Uganda is one country that is showing that this is possible, with early signs of success in its campaign to expand provision and improve access to primary education. The campaign has been developed in line with the National Plan of Action (NPA), drawn up with UNICEF after the 1990 World Summit for Children. The aim is to provide free, universal primary education, beginning with an allocation of up to four children from each household. At independence, Uganda's education system, in common with the rest of its infrastructure, was among the best in Africa, but years of neglect under the Amin and Obote governments caused it to suffer. School fees have previously been a significant disincentive to parents to enrol their children in school, and though enrolment rates are normal by sub-Saharan African standards, the drop-out rate is high. Only 49% of boys and 29% of girls complete primary school, and enrolment rates for secondary school are very low. This gender gap in completion rates reflects the large numbers of girls being withdrawn from school to work, usually in the home, in the poorest areas of the country. There is also a chronic shortage of trained teaching staff, and 40% of primary teachers have no training whatsoever. Nonetheless, teaching quality is still fairly good by regional standards, and parental financial contributions have prevented any further deterioration.

The aim of the 1996/97 budget was to replace these household contributions with government funding, and primary enrolment has almost doubled since then from 2.9 million children to 5.7 million. This rise in numbers has not, however, been met by a commensurate increase in available resources. The student-to-teacher ratio is now almost 80:1, and there is a shortage of classroom space and equipment, particularly books. The commitment to universal education will test the government, especially given revenue shortfalls and budgetary pressures from war-torn parts of the north of the country now back under government control. It is estimated that fulfilling the pledge may cost as much as NUSh200m, more than the military budget. Yet, despite misgivings about the viability of the project, with donor support there is no reason why the targets of the NPA cannot become reality. Debt relief under the conditions of the Heavily Indebted Poor Countries Initiative (HIPC), though far from satisfactory, has led to budget savings of $20m, going some way towards releasing public money for education. The World Bank has provided support for teacher-training programmes and capital expenditure. There is also considerable scope for efficiency improvements on the part of the Ugandan government, which continues to overspend and mis-spend on the military, tertiary education, sophisticated curative health care, and unnecessary bureaucracy.

Raising revenues

Even after public finances have been more equitably and efficiently distributed, and efficiency measures introduced, many countries still need to raise additional resources. Often this will require tax reform, and public bodies capable of efficiently and transparently collecting taxes. Because of the nature of expenditure on health and education, especially its need to increase in line with population growth and income growth, a predictable source of income is needed, and this affects the choice of revenue-raising instruments. Revenue-raising capacities in many developing countries are very weak: the income-tax base is small in predominantly rural non-wage economies; where the average income is low and consumption of non-essentials is restricted to a minority of the population, taxes on production and consumption can fail to raise significant sums. In many countries, tax officials are underpaid and collection systems unduly bureaucratised, making evasion and 'unofficial taxation' attractive to officials, businesses and individual taxpayers. The inefficiency of many developing-country tax systems has often been employed as an argument for enlarging the role of private finance in social provision.

Yet this prognosis is unduly gloomy. Indirect taxes, such as value-added tax, are relatively easy to implement and, if applied carefully, can be progressive. They are also currently under-used in most of the least developed countries where they would be most appropriate. There is also scope for wider use of direct taxes in poor countries, as the case of Uganda has demonstrated. Until recently Uganda had a low level of domestic tax revenue, even by African standards. But since it established a new revenue authority, there have been dramatic fiscal improvements, with the share of GDP collected as revenue rising from 5% to 13% between 1985 and 1996. Current policy is designed to increase direct tax and to cut back on exemptions, though production in the informal sector remains difficult to tax and is a constraint on expanding the revenue base.[51] A spending priority for the government is an increase in teachers' wages and money for school buildings, along with the construction of feeder roads designed to improve market access for rural communities.

The level of tax raised by the state determines not only how much public money is available for social investment, but also what proportion of income reaches the individual household. So the *distribution* of the tax burden has direct consequences for poverty. Often, governments have squeezed the agricultural sector for taxes, rather than upset powerful urban constituencies through high rates of corporation tax, capital gains tax, and progressive income-tax rates, reinforcing the urban–rural disparity in living standards. Regressive taxes designed to pay for public services are not only unjust: they are likely to prove counter-productive, in that they tend only to create even greater need among lower-income groups.

In Latin America especially, income-tax rates have been traditionally low, and regressive indirect taxes have been preferred, hitting directly at the ability of the poor, who spend a larger proportion of their incomes on basic goods and services than upper-income groups, to meet their basic needs. During the 1980s, indirect taxes in Latin America actually rose from 28% to 35% of the total tax burden. In Argentina, a highly urbanised society where the majority of the workforce are in wage labour, only 2% of GDP is collected in income tax, while 9% is collected in VAT.[52] In Brazil less than five per cent of GDP is collected in income tax. In contrast, Indonesia and Malaysia collect almost ten per cent of GDP in income tax, and make more effective use of it in raising the capabilities of the poor. A common argument employed to justify regressive taxes is that low rates of personal taxation for higher-income groups encourage higher levels of savings and investment, whereas progressive taxes punish 'winners' and are a disincentive to wealth creation.

Yet Latin America, with low rates of personal tax, has some of the lowest levels of domestic saving and investment in the world. Mexico's Gross Domestic Savings rate (GDS) in 1993 was 16% of GDP, against 35% in Korea, 35% in Malaysia, and 47% in Singapore. Colombia's GDS was 18% and Brazil's 21%. Meanwhile, private consumption as a proportion of GDP generally exceeds 70% of GDP in Latin America (and reaches 80% in Brazil), whereas in East Asia it is generally below 55% of GDP. The relationship between low levels of personal taxation and economic growth is similarly weak. Releasing the productive potential of the poor through increased educational and market opportunity has a far stronger effect on output than a low rate of personal taxation for the already wealthy. Generally, it is political rather than economic considerations that lead to low personal tax rates and regressive taxation.

Donor support

For countries like Uganda, donor support remains an important source of revenue, allowing the government to start to meet its pledges on achieving universal social-service provision. Falling donor support to poor countries, combined with increased revenue collection, has meant that the share of donor support in developing-country public spending has declined markedly over the last few years. Yet donor support continues to account for a large proportion of total revenues in the least developed countries, where the development challenges are greatest. Considerable attention has been focused in recent years on the harm that aid can do to poor countries, by creating a culture of dependency, causing environmental damage, and being wasted on prestige projects with few long-term benefits. Yet 'bad' or misapplied aid makes a case for good aid, not for no aid.

Where aid is carefully directed, it can have a marked positive impact on growth and poverty reduction. The experience of South Korea is instructive. During the 1950s South Korea was heavily dependent on aid, over a period when access to education was extended to cover the majority of the population. In 1945 only 13.4% of Koreans were literate; by 1960 almost all children were enrolled in primary school, and literacy already stood at 70%. This was in part made possible by huge sums of US aid — larger than those received by any other nation before or since in per capita terms — which promoted self-reliance, not dependence. As the benefits of human-capital investment were felt by South Korea, it was able to develop its comparative advantage and make on-going investments in social provision.

The lessons of South Korea's experience have been lost on the current generation of OECD donors. The World Bank estimates that an overall increase of $10 billion, or 20% of current flows, in aid to developing countries could lift 25 million people out of poverty.[53] Yet development assistance has been cut by 18% since 1990, to its lowest level since the early 1950s, and now stands at around 0.27% of the GDP of the world's richest countries. Much of this is misallocated, being used as a lubricant for trade deals, or being tied to purchases of goods and services from the donor country. Approximately 60% of all aid is spent in the donor country, rather than in the recipient country that it is intended to benefit. Meanwhile, donors continue to underspend on priority social needs. Basic education is a case in point. Only 1.4% of development aid goes to the basic-education sector, despite the fact that tens of millions of children never even begin an education; health spending continues to be similarly neglected.[54] Although it is true that donor support can only ever supplement government expenditures, there is an urgent need for aid to the poorest countries to be both increased and directed to people living in poverty.

Raising demand for social provision

Despite the high private benefits of basic social services, household demand for these services is often low. Raising demand for social provision is as important as (and must happen in tandem with) strategies for increasing the supply of services. There is no single answer to the question of why households so often fail to use basic social services, but demand-side factors are often as significant as state and market failure in explaining poor welfare outcomes. A high level of private demand for social services is crucial to the success of any human-development strategy. Compulsory education is not practicable unless the majority of parents want their children — girls as well as boys — to enrol and attend at school. Improving the health status of a population depends on that population regarding their current health status as unacceptable, and being prepared to alter their behaviour accordingly. Raising household demand is more likely to succeed where people's demands and needs are listened to, and people are enabled to meet them through participatory structures. Often, giving people who live in poverty a genuine opportunity to discuss their needs raises expectations, and raises demand for the rights they are denied.

Data often under-estimate unmet demand

A major problem in distinguishing supply-side and demand-side constraints is the unreliability of data. Often data exaggerate both the level of access and the quality of social-service provision, obscuring the real level of demand that exists for increased investment in social services. Part of the difficulty arises from using figures comparatively, especially in education: definitions of literacy differ from country to country, and often a person is automatically defined as literate after completing only a few years of school. Looking at other indicators, such as the number of newspapers read, gives a clearer impression of functional literacy levels, and suggests that regions such as Latin America with high official literacy rates have fairly low levels of effective literacy.

Similarly, enrolment rates often tell us very little about attendance, and even less about what has been learned. The gross enrolment ratio, the measure of the number of students at a given educational level as a proportion of the students in the age group eligible to attend, conceals large numbers of children outside of school. Whereas the *gross* enrolment rate for girls at primary school in Nepal is 90%, only 40% of girls of primary-school age are actually enrolled. The two principal reasons for the huge disparity between the figures are the high rate of repetition of school years, and the large number of under-age and over-age enrolments.[55] Though this is an extreme case, Nepal is not untypical. Enrolment statistics are also commonly manipulated or exaggerated, often because there are incentives for staff, parents, and officials to do so. For example, a head-teacher's salary may be linked to the number of children enrolled in the school. In India, the 1981 census showed only 47% of 6-11 year-olds attending school, while the internal education-system data — used in official statistics — claimed an enrolment rate of over 80%. Today, the discrepancy between official and actual enrolments remains extremely large.[56] Enrolment and mean years of schooling tell us even less about attainment, since in most countries drop-out rates and repeat years mean that many children end their schooling illiterate and innumerate.

Low-quality social provision is a major factor in declining private demand. For example, low enrolment may reflect reluctance on the part of parents to send their children to poor-quality schools, rather than a shortage of school places. This has happened in Vietnam, where sharp falls in school enrolment have occurred since the late 1980s as quality has deteriorated.[57] Poor-quality services can be difficult to capture statistically, and figures on the proportion of a rural population with access to health services, or the numbers of children registered 'in school', can give the impression that 'health services' means fully equipped and staffed clinics, and 'education' means purpose-built schools. In reality, health and education facilities are often nothing more than an empty, unequipped building. Often developing-country schools are staffed by teachers with only a few years of schooling, while children spend little time being taught, with days lost through staff and student absenteeism shortening already brief school years. The scarcity of basic materials, such as pencils and text books, is a further constraint on successful learning.

In Mozambique, where Oxfam is working with rural communities in Zambezia province to rebuild and equip schools and train teachers after a civil war in which the education and health infrastructure was largely destroyed, each year only 70 cents is spent per pupil on equipment, while the minimum package of books and pencils costs around four dollars. In Colombia, resource misallocation means that secondary schools are so short of funds that most pupils have none of the required textbooks. Country-level statistics can also mask marked regional differences in provisioning. In Campeche and Chiapas, two of Mexico's poorest states, one third of schools provide only three grades of education, in contrast to the seven grades of schooling that Mexicans receive on average.

Low private demand

Clearly, data on social provision do not explain why children remain out of school, or why mortality or morbidity rates are at a certain level. History, culture, ideology, and religion all contribute to welfare outcomes, while it is crucially important to recognise that in social provision the relevant decision makers are not always the consumers. For example, there may be high private returns to primary education, but the costs and benefits are not distributed evenly through the household, and may be not be captured by the parents of the child.

Nor are the private returns to investment in education or health care the same for every social group. Geographically isolated pastoralists, or people from low-status castes in South Asia whose labour-market access is restricted, are unlikely to enjoy the same economic gains from social provision as more privileged social groups. Nor, generally speaking, do women, who are more likely than men to contribute to the household through unpaid labour instead of — or as well as — paid labour. The under-valuing of women's work, and lower levels of female participation in labour markets, are key factors in the gender bias in education access. Two thirds of children in developing countries not enrolled in school are girls. Educating boys often represents a surer form of old-age security than the education of girls, especially in societies where girls are married into another family, and so come to represent a lost investment.

Decisions about girls' education are not based simply on a cost–benefit analysis. The low priority attached by most societies to girls' education reflects powerful customary and ideological forces as well as economic considerations. In many societies, women are viewed as repositories of traditions whose safe transmission to the next generation depends on women's being 'protected' from the alien influences of a modern education. This sense is often strongest where education is not conducted in the local language, as is the case in much of Africa, and in parts of Latin America, such as Peru and Guatemala, where indigenous languages have survived. The skills that a conventional education confers on a child are often seen as unsuitable or irrelevant for girls, especially where the ideal is an early marriage and a life of bearing and rearing children, and household-based labour. A training in household and agricultural skills may be regarded as the best preparation for adult life, rather than the acquisition of literacy and numeracy.

Recession also plays an important part in explaining low private demand for social provision, illustrating the importance of economic growth to achieving and sustaining advances in human welfare. In sub-Saharan Africa, welfare outcomes were affected by the recession of the 1980s, which raised the direct and indirect costs for poor households of using basic services, and reduced both quality and private returns. The 1980s were a period of economic and social decline for all but a handful of African countries, with many of the post-independence economic and social gains wiped out by a decade of slump and conflict.

Nowhere was this reversal of human development more apparent than in the education sector. Per capita education spending in Africa fell by two thirds in real terms between 1980 and 1987,[58] with primary education suffering most, as secondary and tertiary budgets were largely protected. Quality inevitably suffered, at the same time as private returns to schooling diminished. The 1980s were a period of mass lay-offs as state and private enterprises were closed, rationalised, and privatised, and government bureaucracies shrank. The proportion of the population earning a regular wage fell, and with it so did the number of formal-sector income-earning opportunities gained by a basic education. As incomes fell, the hidden costs of education — fees for meals, uniforms, and books — rose in proportion to household income. Opportunity costs also rose. It became increasingly difficult for poor households to keep children in school, when they might be supplementing meagre incomes by peddling goods and services in the burgeoning informal sector.

While economic growth is not a panacea for failure in social provision, it is a necessary basis for raising private demand and extending access. Where income-earning opportunities increase, the private returns to an education become more readily apparent; and where average household incomes rise, the direct and indirect costs generally fall.

Issues of access

Accessible health and education provision is essential if demand is to be raised. Access is not simply about geographical proximity to a resource or facility, as urban welfare indicators in developing countries demonstrate. While coverage of basic social services and access to markets in rural areas are often related to distance, extending access involves other challenges. For example, food is usually available in famine situations, but people go hungry because they do not have the means to buy it. Sick people may fail to take advantage of a health clinic because they are ill-informed about their health-care needs. Four issues of access can be identified as being of particular relevance to the poor:

Affordability

Compulsory education is unlikely to be workable where poor households lose significant potential earnings by keeping their children in school. Often even very modest school fees, textbooks, and uniforms are prohibitively expensive for poor households. There is widespread evidence that the cost of uniforms in particular deters parents from sending children to school. As well as direct costs, there are opportunity costs in sending children to school, rather than keeping them at home to supplement the household income. Similarly, direct and opportunity costs in health care erode access for the poor. Short-term savings, as in education, turn out to incur long-term costs. Poor parents often have to calculate the longer-term benefits to their children and themselves — as a form of old-age security — of completing an education, as against the short-term benefits of entering the labour market. From this point of view, increases in parental income have an instrumental role to play in increasing enrolment and completion rates. In this context, feeding programmes and supplements of iron, iodine, and vitamin A are cheap and effective interventions, represent an important form of income transfer for the poorest households, and can have a significant impact on attendance, enrolment, repetition rates, and performance. As the case study from Mauritania in Box 2.4 demonstrates, feeding programmes can achieve dramatic results in terms of enrolment, attendance, and performance. In Jamaica, free breakfasts for children have improved both attendance and arithmetic results, and in Honduras, *bonos*, or food coupons, distributed to children from the poorest households have led to a marked reduction in repetition rates and an improvement in attendance. Food programmes specifically for girls can be one way of overcoming cultural resistance to female education, and have been used successfully to this end.[59]

Box 2.4 In-school feeding programmes in Mauritania: a case study[60]

In Mauritania, free school meals funded by the World Food Programme have been used successfully to increase enrolment and attendance rates and are believed to have improved the academic performance of the children. In Mauritania, only two thirds of children enrol in school, and drop-out rates are high, especially among girls. Close to 30 per cent of children enrolled in primary school fail to complete five years' primary schooling, and secondary enrolment is only 15%. In line with the UNICEF National Plans of Action (NPAs), the Mauritanian government committed itself to providing universal primary education by the year 2000, and the WFP feeding programme is regarded as an integral part of this. Mauritania's economic health is largely a function of climatic variations, and in periods of low rainfall rural household incomes can drop dramatically, obliging families to withdraw all or some of their children from school. While withdrawal may be seasonal, the education of children suffers from these interruptions to their education. Feeding programmes, first instituted on a small scale over 30 years ago, are a significant incentive to parents to keep their children in school. 45,000 children, most of them in primary education, receive a glass of sweet milk or porridge on arrival in the morning, and a meal at lunchtime. This saves a household the cost of two meals a day — the annual value calculated in 1994 at between 7,000 and 9,5000 *ouguiyas*, or 15% of the minimum rural salary. As well as representing a significant saving to households, the meals are more nutritious and varied than those that most children receive at home, and are estimated to provide more than half the nutritional requirements of the average child.

Low educational attainment is known to be closely connected to food insecurity. Illiteracy, especially among mothers, is a major factor in child malnutrition and in generally low levels of hygiene and health. A key intention of the programme was to enhance educational access for the poorest children, and the impact on enrolment appears to have been positive. The Tarza region, which benefited most from the first stage of the programme implemented in secondary schools, has an exceptionally high enrolment rate of 92%. In recent years, the scheme has been extended to areas where large numbers of people practise nomadic pastoralism, and a marked increase in enrolment levels has followed. The feeding programme has also had an evident impact on attendance levels, especially in sparsely populated areas where children have to travel long distances to school. There is little doubt that a child's capacity to concentrate and assimilate information is affected by his or her diet, though the reports of improvements in children's classroom performance are necessarily more impressionistic. However, teachers have reported lower levels of illness in the classroom as a result of the programme. Ultimately, the success of such schemes is dependent both on a good school system and on parents being convinced of the value of education itself. Feeding programmes need to be part of a co-ordinated scheme designed to generate incentives to persuade parents to take advantage of education provision.

Quality
The net costs of access to social provision are higher where the gains are lower: education is often of a low quality in developing countries, where poorly trained and underpaid staff, high rates of staff absenteeism, lack of evaluation, the absence of a standardised examination system, and the buying of qualifications are common problems. Realistic standards and levels of funding need to be set. Quality demands coherence: fragmented provision, whether commercial or public, leads to wasted resources and makes national strategies less likely to succeed. The damage caused by low-quality education and health care is considerable. It engenders scepticism about the benefits, and resentment of arbitrary and inefficient public interventions. It is unsurprising that parents are reluctant to make significant financial sacrifices to keep their children in run-down schools where they learn very little and leave with few formal labour-market opportunities. Raising demand necessitates raising quality.[61]

Participation
Poverty-reduction strategies are unlikely to succeed unless the people affected are participating in their design, implementation, and evaluation. Adapting interventions to the needs of local communities and target groups, and identifying those needs through participative processes, makes it likelier that poverty-reduction strategies generate *sustainable* change. Participation also fosters higher levels of trust and a greater willingness to co-operate than a system which depends on instructions from above. Because the feedback mechanisms provided by the market are weak or absent in the public sector, a system of institutionalised accountability is essential. Accountability is impossible when the public is ignorant of the costs and performance of public health and education systems. Disseminating information and bringing the community into decision-making roles is therefore central to efforts to maintain efficient and equitable services. In an education or health system, each community or household has its group or individual interests, as well as, usually, a shared interest in the success of the system. Participatory structures can help to avoid factionalism developing and a single-group agenda dominating.

NGOs, including Oxfam, have increasingly emphasised the importance of participation underpinning their project work, and the recognition of the participatory principle is altering the way in which states operate. The case of Ceara, discussed in Box 2.2, illustrates the scope for state structures to work more effectively at the local level by working with and through a wider range of actors than has traditionally been the case. Collaboration between states and 'civil society' also allows consensus to be built about the direction of policy reform, and reduces the likelihood of violent conflict. Where private demand for social services is low, participation has a vital role to play. There is a great deal of scope for decentralisation of resources and responsibility as a way of improving quality and reducing opportunity costs. Innovations such as parent councils and elements of self-funding can increase attendance and improve results. In Mozambique, the government has introduced parent management committees, which have often proved effective in holding schools accountable to the communities they are serving. Yet participation is not a panacea, and the process of empowerment is not a straightforward one, as Box 2.5 shows. Nor are community-based or NGO interventions usually a genuine alternative to state provision. Often decentralisation and participation have been promoted in order to shift costs away from the state on to households, rather than in order to enhance accountability and responsiveness. The central responsibility of the state to ensure that the rights to basic education and health care are respected risks being obscured unless participatory structures are designed as a complement to, rather than a substitute for, state action.

Box 2.5 Parent management committees in Mozambique

Mozambique has some of the world's worst education indicators. More than 60% of children are not enrolled in primary school, quality is poor, and fewer than half of those children who do enrol complete the primary cycle. Most of the education infrastructure was destroyed during the civil war, and there has been a massive reconstruction and rehabilitation programme since the war ended in 1994. Oxfam has been working with local government and rural communities in Zambezia province since the early 1990s, to improve access to primary education. There are numerous challenges in extending access to good-quality education among an overwhelmingly poor and rural population. They are compounded in a part of Mozambique which suffered especially heavily from the long and brutal civil war. Oxfam's education programme has three components: school building, teacher training, and support for parent management committees.

Oxfam support for parent management committees in the eight villages where schools have been built came about through a recognition that one of the best ways of raising educational quality and parental demand was by getting parents actively involved in the life of the school. The LECs (*Ligação Esacola Comunidade*) are recognised in law and encouraged by government. They have a recognised role in helping to maintain and manage school compounds, in monitoring teacher performance, and in providing support for the education of very poor children. In the eight communities where Oxfam has built primary schools, an Oxfam Community Development worker has worked with the committees and organised 'exchange visits', to enable parents to meet committees that are working well.

The record of the LECs in the communities where Oxfam has been working is mixed, with some committees helping to establish genuine school–community partnerships which have improved educational access and quality. In other villages, the committees barely function, and some have been co-opted by corrupt staff. The uneven performance of the LECs offers important lessons for Oxfam and for the education system in Mozambique. In Nipive village, Gurue there is a consensus among parents that the LEC has generated real benefits. There are regular meetings, and the appointments to the LEC change annually. It has enabled parents to challenge policies that result in teachers being transferred to other areas after short periods. They are also pressing for free school meals, textbooks, and pencils, and there are no reports of teacher corruption from parents in the village, a major problem in Mozambique where teachers are poorly and irregularly paid, and school inspections are rare. Thirty miles away, the LEC in Mangone village has a very different track record. The committee organised the construction of the school, but was disbanded afterwards. There are no elections for committee members, and they are not accountable to other parents. The staff in Mangone were reported to charge parents unofficial fees before their children could progress to the next grade, which partly explained the extremely high drop-out and repetition rates. Less than one third of the children who enrol in Mangone are still attending school by the fifth grade.

A key lesson from these experiences is that the social context strongly influences the effectiveness of the committee. In Mangone, most of the population stayed in the village during the civil war, and relations between Frelimo and Renamo supporters have remained polarised. The staff and village leaders have not accepted the principle of working with parents. Many of the villagers are afraid to criticise the staff openly, and corruption is a major problem. In contrast, most of Nipive's population fled the village during the war, either to camps in Malawi or to relatives in government-controlled areas. Many of the parents returned from the camps in Malawi having seen their children receive a basic education, and were keen to continue this when they returned. However, even in Nipive it is the least-poor households, with the best land, and who live nearest to the school, who tend to participate in the committee meetings. The poorest households and those living farthest away from the school are less able to commit time to the LEC. The poorest and most isolated households are also unlikely to have their children enrolled in school. However well they function, the LECs tend to reflect the needs and interests of parents who have children in school, not the parents of unreached learners. Different approaches need to be developed to reach these children and give them new educational opportunities.

Proximity

Most obviously in rural areas, time and effort — and therefore income — spent gaining access to health and education provision is a major determinant of the standard of living. Children who have to walk several miles to school spend longer away from the home, so that the opportunity costs are higher, and they have greater nutritional requirements than children who have only a short distance to travel. One survey in Egypt found that where a school was one kilometre away, male enrolment was 94% and female enrolment was 72%. Where the school was two kilometres away, boys' enrolment dropped to 90%, and girls' enrolment to 64%. In rural Africa, most school facilities are over two kilometres away. One reason why proximity appears to have a much greater impact on girls' enrolment than on boys' is that many parents believe girls will be exposed to moral and physical dangers if they travel long distances for their education.[62]

Distance is a factor in the use of health facilities in much the same way as it is with education. Often, mobile services — such as travelling immunisation clinics — are a way of reaching marginalised rural communities. Mobile services can also be important in urban areas. The urban poor often live in shanty settlements without formal legal recognition, lacking basic health and education facilities, while transport costs are often high. In all cases, responding to social demand, rather than leaving the market to respond to effective demand, is the key to equitable access.

Social provision: policy guidelines for equity, poverty reduction, and growth

The widely disparate health and education outcomes achieved by countries at similar income levels, and under similar political conditions, leave us with at least one unambiguous lesson: universal social provision is not an unaffordable luxury, even for governments working from the most limited resource base. States can learn from their own and others' mistakes and successes in social provisioning, and become more successful in reducing poverty and increasing opportunity. For this to happen, equity needs to be put at the top of the public-policy agenda: needs, not privilege, must dictate the forms that provision takes, if rapid developmental growth is going to be achieved. Five policy guidelines can be identified.

Equitable access

Poverty eradication depends on providing education and health services that poor people can afford to use, in terms of both direct and opportunity costs, and services that are worth using. Schools where nothing is learned, and hospitals without medicines or qualified staff, are of little use to anybody. Equitable access demands sufficient and efficient investment in basic services.

Emphasis on basic services

Equitable access to social provision depends on governments protecting and prioritising basic services. Experience would suggest that the governments of least-developed countries generally need to spend five per cent or more of national income on education, and two per cent or more on health, to achieve schooling for all at the primary level and universal basic health-care coverage. As has been shown, throwing money at social services in itself guarantees nothing. Budgets need to be strongly biased in favour of basic services for the poor, where the social returns are greatest. At the same time, management and administrative capacity needs to be developed, to ensure that public spending is efficiently and effectively used. The poorest countries ought, at current spending levels, to be committing the majority of their education budgets to primary schooling. While it is unrealistic to leave the secondary and tertiary sectors simply to respond to effective demand, private finance may be necessary where resources are constrained. In health, spending should be focused on preventative treatments, which in the long term are far more cost-effective than curative care.

Public spending on basic services

The market mechanism does not deliver public goods efficiently and equitably. Basic services that have a high public-goods content require public action to protect access for the poor. There is both a moral responsibility on the part of the state to protect the basic rights of its citizens and a long-term economic interest in a healthy and educated population. A shift away from out-of-pocket payments in developing countries is needed, with basic needs met through the state. Mothers and young children should be treated as priority groups. Until or unless basic rights are respected, only a minimum of public money should be invested in secondary and tertiary education and sophisticated curative health care. Obviously, sufficient investment in higher-level social provision is needed to produce competent schoolteachers, civil servants, and doctors. What is important is that a balance is struck, and that spending patterns reflect need rather than the interests of powerful constituencies.

An end to waste

Public money in the developing world is frequently mis-spent and misappropriated on an enormous scale. While corruption is not confined to developing countries, it carries higher opportunity costs for the poor when resources are scarce. Prestige projects, such as Nigeria's new capital at Abuja, or India's space programme, not only reflect distorted political priorities. They are also closely connected to the abysmal record of social provision in these countries, which between them account for the deaths of ten thousand children every day. In Kenya, an estimated $500 million has been expropriated from public funds through a single import-exemption scheme, more than double the annual expenditure on public health.[63] Non-productive spending on the military is similarly wasteful, though less spectacular. While military expenditure is not wholly discretionary, many of the poorest countries continue to spend at levels that are inconsistent with poverty-reduction aims. Similarly, spending on parastatal subsidisation would yield far higher social returns if it were diverted into social investment and training programmes for laid-off workers.

International action

- *Donor support* should be increased from its current and declining levels, and redirected towards meeting basic needs in the least developed countries. Currently, the LLDCs receive less than one quarter of all Overseas Development Assistance. Donor governments should end the abuse of ODA as a lubricant for trade and commit their budgets explicitly to poverty eradication. At least 20 per cent of ODA should be used for basic social services. ODA currently stands at its lowest levels since the 1950s. An increase from its current level of 0.27% of OECD GDP to the 0.7% level recommended by the United Nations would release an additional $95 billion dollars which, spent wisely, could yield dramatic results in human development. Donors currently below the UN threshold should set a target of annual increases in ODA, reaching 0.7% within the next decade.

■ *Debt relief* should be extended and the existing initiatives should be deepened and accelerated, with the budget savings committed to future social investment. The IMF–World Bank Heavily Indebted Poor Country initiative is a welcome departure from previous debt-relief initiatives, but remains inadequate, given the scale of unmet basic needs in the most indebted poor countries. The current framework has set the completion of two successive IMF adjustment programmes over a six-year period as a precondition of relief, meaning that relief is slow in coming. No mechanism has been developed to ensure that people living in poverty actually benefit, and the relief on offer remains in most cases modest. Oxfam believes that a more flexible and generous approach is required, which focuses on government commitment to poverty reduction and the capacity to use savings from debt relief effectively.

3 Livelihoods

Labour, equity, and poverty eradication

Economic growth is crucial for poverty eradication, but it is insufficient by itself. The previous two chapters have shown that the way in which growth is *distributed* determines whether or not growth is 'developmental', enabling people to lead better, freer, and more worthwhile lives. Economic growth facilitates poverty eradication — in the broad sense of expanding capabilities – only where poor people are equipped with the means to participate in that growth, rather than left to depend on the possible benefits of growth trickling down to them. This is one reason why Oxfam believes the basic rights to health and education are important, as the previous chapter illustrated. Investing in the provision of health care and education can empower people who are marginalised and deprived, and expand their livelihood opportunities.

However, investing in social provision alone will not deliver equitable growth. For 'equality of opportunity' to mean anything, opportunities must be there to be grasped. The World Bank has long been an advocate of labour-intensive growth in developing countries. But labour-intensive growth by itself is no guarantee of a route out of poverty. For that to happen, growth must be 'pro-poor', generating new, viable opportunities for people in poverty to secure the right to a livelihood in a way that does not infringe on their other basic rights. 'Pro-poor labour-intensive growth' requires the equitable and efficient social provision discussed in the last section. But it also demands the development of new trade and employment regimes, which re-establish control over capital, and subordinate markets to the end of meeting social need. This chapter examines the role of livelihood opportunities in poverty eradication, and the policy measures that are needed to achieve pro-poor and labour-intensive growth.

Labour and livelihoods: some basic concepts

Our assets, and the returns we are able to command in exchange for our labour are the two crucial determinants of poverty and inequality levels.

Labour is the key asset of the poor: among the poorest people are those who have nothing to sell but their labour and still cannot find a regular buyer. So poverty eradication entails equipping the poor with the means to increase the returns on their labour. This can be done only by coordinating social-provision and livelihood strategies. The development experience of countries such as Brazil, discussed in Chapters 1 and 2, demonstrates that unchecked growth will not automatically benefit the poorest people, or create viable income-earning opportunities. There is 'directed', labour-intensive growth, and there is wasted growth, which fails to translate into efficient poverty reduction. Creating new livelihood opportunities is also good for equity, and so for growth. In a market economy, economic benefits are distributed principally through the labour market. Generally, the greater the proportion of the working-age population participating in the labour market, and the greater the proportion of value-added taken by wages, the more equitable is the distributive outcome, and the greater the level of aggregate demand.

Creating livelihood opportunities involves more than employment creation, although this is an important dimension of poverty-eradication strategies. This is because few people, especially among the poor, have a single 'job' on which they are dependent for their survival. Instead, the majority of people, in the urban 'informal' sector[1] and in rural areas, tend to survive by a number of strategies. In most societies the typical household holds a diverse 'portfolio' of economic activities, and often no one individual fits a single occupational category. This is especially the case in developing countries, where the formal sector of the economy is often small. Increasingly, the term 'livelihood' better captures the 'complex and diverse reality' of poor people's economic activities.[2] Discovering ways of making livelihoods sustainable and more likely to deliver an acceptable standard of living is an urgent priority for governments and organisations committed to poverty eradication.

Much of Oxfam's work – for example, offering farmers in the Sahel advice and equipment so they can irrigate their crops rather than depend on unpredictable rainfall; giving a fair and predictable price to coffee co-operatives in Central America; or supporting credit schemes in Pakistan which give poor women the opportunity to set up small businesses — is about making livelihoods more secure. The more secure people are, the better able they are to plan for the future by saving and investing. Planning for the future reduces the vulnerability of households — to a food-price increase, a tropical storm, or a rise in the cost of sending a child to school — which so often pushes people back into the poverty trap.

Reducing vulnerability to poverty, and reducing poverty itself, requires expanding the effective freedoms available to poor people. In the urban informal sector, this may require the abolition of petty controls on street trading, such as licensing systems, which create scope for rent-seeking by public officials, and the provision of equitable and efficient public transport. In rural areas, a choice of crop varieties and access to credit are two strategies that can greatly enhance the quality of life. Some of these options will be discussed later in this chapter.

Developing sustainable livelihoods is viable even in poor countries where growth is slow or negative. Although rapid economic growth is important to employment creation, strategies that promote sustainable livelihoods are possible in low-growth and no-growth environments, and in the short to medium term are imperative in those countries where rapid economic growth remains elusive. In the Indian state of Maharashtra, the 'Employment Guarantee Scheme' is one example of how livelihoods can be made more secure by modest state interventions against a backdrop of low growth. Guaranteed employment during periods of food shortages and seasonal underemployment helped to revive the rural economy and improve the terms of employment for labourers.[3]

The costs of underutilised labour

Because the capacity to secure a livelihood is a basic human need, underemployment and unemployment carry obvious psychological costs for the individual. The costs of underutilised labour are felt by a landless Brazilian family unable to meet their needs from the income generated by the roadside verge they cultivate; and by unemployed workers in the deprived urban areas of Britain whose skills and age leave them with no real prospect of another job. But the costs to society at large of denying substantial numbers of people the right to a viable livelihood are often ignored, or even denied. This is a mistake, and the psycho-social impact of unemployment and underemployment is increasingly being recognised. The growing use by the United Nations Development Programme of unemployment figures as an index of social cohesion for industrialised societies is a recognition of the social impact of wasted labour.[4]

People whose skills are utilised and valued by their society, and who are remunerated fairly, are able not only to meet their basic material needs, but also have a stake in a stable and prosperous society. People who are able to make an economically meaningful contribution are also likely to contribute more broadly to civil society. Genuinely participatory political cultures depend on a widespread feeling of inclusion and

91

relative equality. It is not surprising that in the industrialised countries the long-term unemployed and the low-paid are far less likely to vote than those in higher-income groups. Wasted labour is socially destabilising, leaving people feeling abused and undervalued and often with little to lose from violent or criminal behaviour.

In Peru the implosion of the formal economy in the late 1980s led to record levels of unemployment, with the International Labour Organisation estimating total underemployment to exceed 70%. The success of the extremist Shining Path guerrillas was fuelled in part by the resentment of landless peasants and unemployed workers who felt they had been ignored by mainstream political parties. Thirty thousand people died in a conflict that further impoverished the countryside and placed new pressures on the urban infrastructure, as an estimated 600,000 people fled rural areas for the safety of cities.[5] In neighbouring Bolivia, the hectarage of coca under cultivation increased dramatically after 1985, when 20,000 tin miners were laid off. Many felt their best chance of security would come from spending their redundancy payments on plots of land and coca seed. Though the money to be made by the growers was unspectacular, the cartels offered stable prices, in sharp contrast to the fluctuating prices for licit commodity crops. The attendant cost, however, was spiralling rural violence and administrative corruption. Today, perhaps 40 per cent of Bolivians are economically dependent, directly or indirectly, on coca.[6]

These social and political costs generate economic costs. The price paid for wasted labour is obvious in a developed economy with an extensive social-security system, where the bill for supporting the unemployed is typically one of the largest items of public expenditure. In Least Developed Countries, where underutilised labour does not necessarily imply a direct fiscal drain on government, the costs are more likely to be ignored. Yet both in the North and South, underutilised labour costs economies huge sums in lost potential output. Moreover, underutilised labour is low-income labour, and contributes little to aggregate demand for goods and services. In other words, it tends to feed into a cycle of low growth or no growth.

Growth, distribution, and income-earning opportunities

Rapid and sustained economic growth is important, because it tends to expand the range of income-earning opportunities for the poor. Yet, though important, growth is not a guarantee of expanded opportunities. A characteristic trend of the world economy over the last two decades has been the weakening of the relationship between GDP growth and employment creation, and the emergence of the phenomenon of 'jobless growth'. Often this is partly accounted for by growth in capital-intensive primary-commodity production, which creates few employment opportunities, or (as in many Northern countries) by the introduction of labour-displacing technologies. Meanwhile in many developing countries that have liberalised their economies, privatisation programmes can generate growth, while often leading simultaneously to large-scale lay-offs.

While some of the most successful developing economies of the last three decades, from Botswana to Taiwan, have combined rapid GDP growth with higher rates of employment growth than labour-force growth, many developing countries have been better at generating growth than jobs. In India, from 1979 to 1989, annual employment growth rates of 2% lagged behind GDP growth rates of around 5%. In Ghana between 1986 and 1991, while GDP grew by an average of 4.8%, employment fell by more than 13%.[7] It cannot be taken for granted that growth will deliver new income-earning opportunities for the poor, or deliver them at the rate that is needed to reduce poverty.

For this to happen, two approaches are needed. Firstly, there is a need for equitable and efficient social investment, an area in which countries such as India and Ghana have a poor record. Second, targeting sectors in which growth is labour-intensive, including agriculture, which is discussed below, can make a significant impact on poverty levels. Many of the developing countries with a successful record in job-creation have targeted strategic labour-intensive sectors, with the real wage bill growing at a rapid rate and income distribution improving.

With the emergence of the phenomenon of 'jobless growth', the consensus that full employment is viable or, indeed, desirable was broken. Many economists argue the benefits of a small pool of surplus labour, keeping wages down and weakening the disruptive effects of collective labour bargaining. The evidence for this thesis is weak, however. Making labour-costs the keystone of an employment strategy is misguided, since low-cost labour is generally low-productivity labour. The experience of the UK is a case in point, where between the mid-1980s and mid-1990s there was greater deregulation of its labour market than in any other EU member state. Union rights were curtailed and minimum-wage protection was withdrawn, with the aim of creating employment and fostering international competitiveness. Yet the majority of new jobs that were created were in low-productivity — and therefore low-wage —

areas of the service sector. From 1985 to 1994, the UK had the lowest per capita GNP growth rate in the EU. The growth that did take place was not distributed equitably, because it was not based on rising productivity, and therefore rising real wages, among the poor. The one indicator that did register dramatic growth during the 1980s was the level of income inequality, which rose faster than at any time since the last century.[8]

Labour costs per unit of output, rather than labour costs themselves, are the relevant factor in investment decisions. A corollary of this is that competitiveness is shaped far more by human-capital levels than by wage levels, and the most successful economies with the highest rates of poverty reduction and the best record on income inequality over the last two decades have been those countries that have invested in their human-capital stock, making possible growth based on rising productivity. And labour-productivity increases tend to have an equalising effect on income distribution, because gains are translated into real wage increases. In contrast, basing competitive advantage on low labour costs is a circuitous, as well as less just, route out of poverty.

One reason for East Asia's high poverty-reduction elasticity of growth, discussed in the first chapter, is that economic growth in the region has been labour-intensive and based on goods with higher added value, often destined for expanding export markets. One per cent of manufacturing growth in Malaysia or Indonesia produces twice the number of jobs that the same rate does in Brazil or India. In Taiwan and South Korea, where rapid growth and full employment were achieved, knowledge-based industries have been promoted, with rising productivity leading to further investment and new jobs. Export-oriented manufacturing growth in Taiwan and South Korea was emulated by the newly industrialised countries (NICs) of the second tier, and Malaysia and Thailand increased the share of manufactures in their total exports more than tenfold over just 25 years. The fall over the same period in the industrialised countries' share of global manufacturing value-added is accounted for almost entirely by the growth of export manufacturing in the East Asian region. In per capita terms, the regional value of all exports rose by 14% a year during the 1990s, in comparison with 7% for Latin America. The composition of exports is closely correlated to these trends. As Figure 3.1 shows, the rise of manufacturing value-added as a proportion of GDP in major East Asian economies has been paralleled by a diminished role for manufactures in the exports of major Latin American and sub-Saharan African economies.

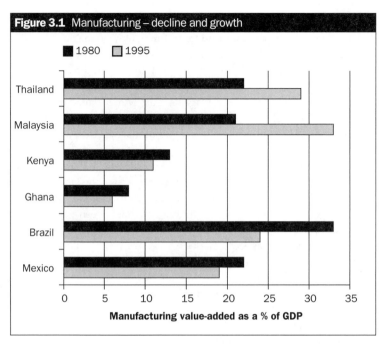

Figure 3.1 Manufacturing – decline and growth

■ 1980 ☐ 1995

Manufacturing value-added as a % of GDP

In contrast to the export-oriented use of protective controls in the NICs, Import Substituting Industrialisation in Brazil led to various unintended disincentives against labour-intensive investment. Protections and subsidies were applied indiscriminately, with perverse consequences. Restrictions on imports made many basic technologies from overseas which would have improved productivity rates prohibitively expensive, while a lack of local competition often kept supplier prices artificially high. Overvalued exchange rates have been a common feature of Latin American economies in the last few decades, used partly as a device to maintain the political support of the wealthiest sections of society. Yet they also had the effect of making labour-intensive manufactures uncompetitive in export markets, and acted as an incentive to substitute an abundant labour supply with imported manufacturing equipment. In traditional commodity-export sectors, meanwhile, antagonistic labour relations led to labour-saving technologies being adopted. One result of capital-intensive growth in Latin America has been that the socially destabilising inequalities in income, health care, and education in the region have continued to widen. The poor have continued to be excluded from the growth process.

The working poor

While unemployment and underemployment are major causes of poverty, employment creation is not a panacea for poverty. In many developing countries, a significant proportion of households belong to the 'working poor'. Formal-sector employment is commonly failing to pay a living wage, as minimum-wage laws are either flouted or rendered meaningless by inflation. Nor are the working poor confined to the South. In the USA, increasingly parsimonious welfare payments are forcing many of the least skilled to accept wages that leave them no better off in work than out of it. Because of low skill levels — the principal reason why the long-term unemployed were outside the labour market in the first place — there is little income-group mobility among the working poor, and labour-productivity growth has been negligible.[9] If poverty eradication was the intended aim of the squeeze on welfare, it has so far not been achieved.

In Chile, the working poor now account for such a large section of the economically active population that low wages are the single most important cause of poverty. Two thirds of adults below the poverty line used by the UN Economic Commission for Latin America are in employment, and between 1990 and 1992 the share of national income allocated to wages actually fell. This fall had a disproportionate impact on lower-income groups: over the same period, the income share of the wealthiest population decile remained at 45%.[10] Clearly, in Chile job creation has not been an automatic escape route from poverty. Oxfam has worked since the early 1970s in Chile, supporting workers in the garment and shoe industries for whom rapid economic growth has instead spelt growing insecurity and poverty wages. While the country's impressive growth record in recent years is in sharp contrast to those of its Latin American neighbours, the benefits of wealth creation have bypassed the most marginal groups in society.

The working poor in Chile suffer from insecurity as well as poverty wages. Work, especially in agricultural exports, is seasonal, and employees' basic rights are rarely observed. This 'hire and fire' culture limits the ability of the workers to save, spread risks, plan, and invest. In short, it prevents them escaping from the poverty trap. Again, the experience of Chile is a reminder of the importance of linking the right to a livelihood to other basic rights: two thirds of wage labour is employed on a temporary basis, double the level in 1980, and piece rates, limited or non-existent union rights, minimal social-security protection, and no sickness or maternity rights are the rule rather the exception.

Creating income-earning opportunities: means and ends

Employment creation, like growth, is a means to the end of increasing human welfare. If the object of creating new livelihood opportunities is the expansion of human capabilities, then the kind of employment culture that is created is crucially important. Too often, labour-intensive growth is more anti-poor than anti-poverty. The USA may have been relatively successful in reducing unemployment, but has been conspicuously unsuccessful in reducing levels of inequality and violent crime. If the two per cent of US men currently imprisoned, and the further four per cent on parole are added to the unemployment statistics, unemployment levels are comparable to those in many Western European countries. It may be partly true that for the poor the one thing worse than having their labour exploited is not to have their labour exploited. Yet it is also irrelevant, since labour-market regulation that protects basic rights is efficient, as well as fair. Exploited labour in unregulated labour markets is less productive, and the costs in terms of efficiency as well as equity are considerable.

Again, the experience of Taiwan is instructive, demonstrating that equitable, labour-intensive growth based on a constant upgrading of skills is feasible. Taiwan combined low wage differentials, per capita growth rates of 8% and near-full employment over several decades. Until recently, countries such as Sweden and Japan also enjoyed rapid growth, low levels of inequality, and near-full employment, demonstrating that growth and equity are not necessarily mutually exclusive. The experience of countries that have succeeded in combining growth with equity offers an important lesson: the right to a livelihood entails just and favourable working conditions and cannot be isolated from other rights.

Urbanisation and the changing face of poverty

Urbanisation

A fundamental change in the way people live has taken place over the last 40 years; it is altering the profile of poverty and posing new challenges to organisations committed to poverty reduction. Hundreds of millions of people in the last four decades have left the countryside in search of a better standard of living in the city. The ways in which people secure a livelihood have changed radically as a result. As Table 3.1 shows, the proportion of people securing a livelihood on the land has fallen by 15% in 25 years, while the proportion of people engaged in manufacturing has also fallen. Increasingly we are dependent on selling goods and services to each other. In a services-based world, human capital will assume an ever more central role in establishing competitive advantage. In the city, a lack of human capital affects the ability to secure a livelihood more directly than it does in the countryside.[11]

This demographic shift from countryside to city has been so large that in the early years of the twenty-first century, for the first time in human history, more people will live in urban areas than in the countryside. Whereas in 1960 one third of the world's population lived in cities, today just under half do, the figure made artificially low by the huge rural populations of China and India, which account for more than 50% of the developing world's rural population. In 1960 the largest cities were in the North, and almost all developing countries were predominantly rural. Today, Latin America is more urbanised than the industrial countries, as is the East Asian region, if China is excluded. Eight of the world's ten largest cities are in developing countries, and the towns and cities in developing countries are continuing to grow at more than double the rate of overall population increase.[12]

In 1960 poverty was overwhelmingly a rural phenomenon. Development agencies, academics, and governments focused their attention and resources on tackling issues such as access to land, food security, and agricultural modernisation. While poverty is still deepest and most pervasive in the rural South, and the Least Developed Countries remain predominantly rural, the urbanisation of the developing world has led to urban poverty on a scale unknown 40 years ago. The change is significant, not least because, in an increasingly urbanised and market-oriented world, the relationship between poverty, inequality, and labour-market status is stronger than ever before: the urban poor tend to be those with low and irregular incomes and few formal labour rights.

Table 3.1 World output and labour force by sector (%)

(Source: ILO, World Employment 1995)

	Output 1960	Output 1990	Labour force 1965
Agriculture	10.4	4.4	57
Industry	28.4	21.4	19
Services	50.4	62.4	24

Urban living poses problems of access quite different from those in rural areas. The extent of urban poverty tends to be underestimated in official reports by the World Bank and UN: household surveys reveal far higher levels of urban poverty than are suggested by income lines, since the income needed to avoid poverty in cities is far greater than in rural areas.[13] Urban living tends to carry many hidden costs, from poor air quality and associated health problems, to the need to pay for transport. 'Urban poverty' itself is ill-defined, since the basic needs of the city dweller are both more varied and less readily identifiable than those of the peasant household which is dependent principally on one productive asset — land — plus the relevant inputs. For example, the increased importance of literacy in an urban labour market may impoverish the new arrival whose low educational attainment mattered little as a smallholder farmer. A substantial amount of rural poverty is effectively transferred to the city in this way by assetless and unskilled migrants. Deteriorating physical infrastructure, high levels of violent crime, and a surplus unskilled labour supply conspire to place a downward pressure on living standards in many cities in the South, creating new stresses. In the *favelas* of Recife in Brazil, home to 700,000 people, migrants from rural areas — many of them landless and unable to secure a livelihood in the countryside — have built ramshackle homes from plastic, wood, and metal on low-lying swamps without drainage or basic amenities. Oxfam works with community groups in the *favelas*, where the stresses of urban living have contributed to widespread mental-health problems. In turn, these have been a factor in exceptionally high marital breakdown rates. One result is that the proportion of households below the government poverty line headed by women has doubled to almost 30% in the last 20 years.[14] The urban poverty trend has forced governments, inter-national agencies, and NGOs, including Oxfam, to reconsider their anti-poverty strategies, as urban unemployment and under-employment increasingly influence both overall poverty levels and the nature of poverty. Social exclusion, as well as material poverty, takes new forms in the urban context.

Labour migrancy, livelihoods, and living standards

Migration from the countryside to the city takes place for a variety of reasons. Historically, as countries have developed, they have urbanised, with the demand for labour in the cities attracting people from the countryside. Because labour productivity is generally higher in manufacturing than in agriculture, incomes in urban areas are also higher and there is greater social mobility, attracting people in search of an improved standard of living. As well as the 'pull' factors drawing people to cities, there are 'push' factors which encourage migration from rural areas. These push factors are strongest where there is widespread rural impoverishment and underemployment: the lower the standard of living in the countryside, the greater the volume of migration to the cities. Migration alters the countryside as well as the city, since the city is the principal market for rural products. Those people who stay in the countryside often diversify their 'portfolio of activities' by sending a household member to the city, either temporarily or permanently. Increasingly, rural communities look to improve or maintain their standard of living by securing livelihoods in the city.

In most developing countries, migrant labour plays a major role in supporting rural communities. In Southern Africa, for several generations men from rural areas have gone to work in the region's mines, supplementing rural household incomes. Few families in rural Mexico do not have a member in a major Mexican or US city, often sending back remittances and goods to the home village. Yet despite the benefits of migration, both for the migrants and the communities they leave behind, the social costs are often considerable. All too often, migration leads to new forms of vulnerability, dependency, poverty, and exploitation. The breakdown of traditional family structures can be precipitated by separation, with women often left to cultivate land and bring up children single-handedly. The migrants who leave the countryside tend to be the most skilled, and communities can be left populated only by the most vulnerable groups: the young, the old, and the least educated. In certain instances, the effect of migration can be a deepening, rather than reduction, of rural poverty. Migration exacts social as well as economic costs, with the increasing traffic between village and city often eroding local culture. Institutions which gave people a valuable sense of cultural identity can disappear as a society becomes more mobile, and often this leads to alienation between generations. The new-found social mobility can carry even graver consequences in the form of HIV-AIDS, brought back to rural areas by migrant labour. In sub-Saharan Africa, miners and traders returning home to villages have contributed to the devastating spread of the virus, as have East Asian sex workers returning from migrant work in Thailand.[15]

Box 3.1 Industrialisation in Mexico's maquiladora zone

Endemic poverty and violence in rural Mexico have propelled migration from the countryside for generations, reinforced today by the militarisation of rural Chiapas and Guerrero and the growing regional disparities in wealth in the wake of the signing of the North American Free Trade Agreement (NAFTA) in 1994. Under the terms of NAFTA, a ban on US maize imports was withdrawn, along with a range of price supports for small maize farmers, accounting for one third of the value of the domestic maize output. More than two million maize producers are affected by this loss of protection: US imports, from farms with productivity levels four times higher than their Mexican counterparts, are forcing many Mexicans to migrate North to the USA and the border area's *maquiladora* (assembly) industries in search of employment. NAFTA liberalised trade and investment between Mexico, the USA, and Canada, leading hundreds of US manufacturers to relocate parts of their production operations to sprawling border conurbations such as Mexicali and Ciudad Juárez, which only 50 years ago were sleepy provincial towns. Hundreds of thousands of jobs have been created, and remittances from *maquiladora* workers have become especially important to rural communities whose incomes have fallen in the aftermath of agricultural liberalisation in the mid-1980s. Since then, 40% of small agricultural businesses have failed in Mexico.[16] Though wages in the *maquiladoras* average about one dollar an hour, in the context of the high underemployment levels since 1994 and the strong downward pressure on labour costs (in Mexico, 6.7 million people entered the labour market between 1988 and 1995, yet only one million new formal-sector jobs were created[17]), the *maquiladoras* have had no difficulty in attracting migrant labour.

Though the *maquiladoras* have created employment opportunities, the booming border zone is a classic case of labour-intensive growth often being more anti-poor than anti-poverty. The experiences of migrant workers who move to the border towns illustrate many of the dilemmas and stresses faced by the urban poor throughout the developing world. Wages that are one tenth or less of those paid to US workers may be prized by a rural migrant from Chiapas for whom the alternative is continuing impoverishment, violence, and hunger in the countryside, but there are hidden costs for the new arrivals. Shanty towns have grown up around the factories without any planning. Conditions for many new migrants are squalid, with households lacking basic sanitation or drainage, and the dirt streets serving as open sewers, spreading hepatitis and tuberculosis. The air is often difficult to breathe and the water toxic, and there is little in the way of environmental tests. Many US companies are drawn south by the weak environmental and labour regulations in the region, knowing that the controls that do reach the statute books are only weakly enforced. The environmental costs are borne instead by workers. Cases have been reported of women assembling electronic components suffering high blood pressure, headaches, eye infections, and brain haemorrhages as a result of constant exposure to lead fumes.[18] In Matamoros, the incidence of anencephalic births, where babies are born without brains, is 30 times the national average, the result of unrestricted toxic discharges into the Rio Grande.[19] Labour rights are treated with similar contempt. Human-rights groups have reported instances of women employed by multinational corporations including Siemens, Samsung, and Pacific Dunlop being forced to undergo pregnancy tests as a condition of employment.[20] Meanwhile attempts to organise labour for improved pay and conditions are routinely met with dismissal and suppression, in clear contravention of Articles 20 and 23 of the Universal Declaration of Human Rights — part of a pattern of labour repression that, according to the International Confederation of Free Trade Unions (ICFTU), is on the increase in competitive export industries throughout the South. In 1994, one hundred workers at the Chihuahua plants of General Electric and Honeywell, two US-owned multinationals, were laid off for attempting to organise or participating in union activities.

Whether or not many foreign investors in Mexico would act on their threats to relocate in the event of the introduction of more stringent labour regulations is unclear. Mexico is already unable to compete with Haiti and the Central American republics purely on the basis of labour costs, and the threats appear to have been effective in cementing a compact between the Mexican government and foreign investors to keep employment rights to an absolute minimum. Low wages and a high turnover of labour make organising effective labour representation a difficult task, and where official unions (principally the CTM, or Confederation of Mexican Workers, attached to the ruling party, PRI) are permitted, labour–employer relations are characterised by co-option rather than co-operation.[21]

In contrast to the experience of the Mexican border towns (see Box 3.1), urbanisation has often taken place *without* industrialisation. The classical model of economic development, where surplus rural labour is absorbed by the urban industrial sector — invested in by the accumulated capital generated through agricultural modernisation – does not apply in much of the developing world. Nigeria's experience is a case in point. In 1960, 86% of Nigeria's population lived in rural areas, with industry accounting for 10% of the labour force, concentrated in Ibadan and Lagos.

Today more than 50 million Nigerians, 43% of the population, live in urban areas, with industry as a sector now employing 7% of the labour force. Urbanisation has continued to accelerate despite the collapse of the manufacturing sector outside a few key extractive industries. In Nigeria, as in most of sub-Saharan Africa, for the last two decades new jobs in the formal sector have not been created at the same rate as new workers have entered the wage-labour market.

This pattern has been repeated across much of the South over the last 20 years. Jobs lost in their millions during the severe recession of the 1980s (the 'lost decade', when a largely inefficient and mainly urban state sector was dismantled across Latin America and Africa) have not been replaced. Despite modest economic recovery in many countries since the early 1990s, wages have not reached pre-crisis levels, and insufficient jobs have been generated. Those who kept their jobs through the 1980s saw wage levels free-fall, their real purchasing power reduced to 1960s levels by shock devaluations. Deflationary economic policies were allied to social-sector cost-recovery policies — both of which were promoted by the Bretton Woods institutions as mainstays of the stabilisation and restructuring process. Usually this led to painfully counterproductive results. The urban poor were faced with a price–income squeeze, as the effects of unemployment and downward pressure on wages were compounded by the marketisation of public goods. The majority of new recruits to the labour market were left with underemployment in the informal sector as the only option left open to them, the absence of state supports in most developing countries meaning that few can afford to be fully unemployed.

While formal unemployment is not a major cause of poverty in most least-developed countries, underutilised labour is pervasive. In the cities of the developing countries, and in Latin America and Africa in particular, rapid population growth and the collapse of the formal sector in the 1980s led to a massive expansion of what came to be called the 'informal sector'. Though ill-defined, the informal sector is generally characterised by small-scale, household-based, insecure, legally unrecognised, and untaxed work. The informal sector, unlike the black market in a planned economy, is integrally linked to the formal sector: many informal-sector enterprises sell services and goods to the formal sector, and subcontracting out to the informal sector by formal-sector firms is commonplace in services such as refuse-collection. Of course, the informal sector is not a new phenomenon, but the numbers dependent upon it for their survival soared in the 1980s and 1990s. Rural violence and declining terms of trade for agricultural products pushed migration to the cities, while urban bureaucrats and parastatal workers were laid off in their hundreds of thousands. In cities such as Managua, Lima, Kinshasa, and Cairo, over half of the labour force is by most estimates engaged in selling basic services and goods under these conditions. According to some economists, the informal sector is a positive development. Petty traders have been celebrated as examples of entrepreneurial initiative in the face of adversity. Unencumbered by taxation and state interference, they operate in conditions of near-perfect competition, building up a new economic base and rendering the old formal economy and state strategies redundant.[22]

Yet work in the informal sector is often little more than an *ad hoc* survival strategy forced upon the most vulnerable groups in society — rural migrants, unskilled women, children, and disabled people — characterised by their poor skill levels and low social status. At best, livelihoods in the informal sector are a partial solution to the problems posed by a shrinking formal sector, with tens of millions of the urban poor eking out a more or less marginal existence shining shoes, collecting garbage, washing cars, and selling snack food, stolen goods, and household manufactures.

As the ranks of informal workers have increased, their incomes have fallen. The urban poor have suffered a squeeze on their purchasing power and capabilities on two sides. The loss of state-sector jobs during the 1980s exerted a downward pressure on wages in the urban formal sector, reducing average purchasing power. Yet simultaneously the numbers working in the informal sector increased, crowding it out. The necessities of survival have dictated that demand be met by oversupply: too many street vendors chasing too few customers has led to declining incomes among informal-sector workers. Between 1980 and 1991, average incomes in the informal sector declined by between 23.5% and 39.3% in Costa Rica, Brazil, Argentina, and Peru, from what were already low levels.[23] Cholera returned on a significant scale to Latin America, soup kitchens filled up, and crime levels escalated.

The growth of the informal sector in most developing countries has had further negative impact by eroding the tax base of governments. The difficulties of taxing the income and profits of small-scale, household-based or street-based enterprises in the grey and black economies are a factor in the growing dependence on often regressive taxes on consumption and trade.[24] Increasingly, the state in many LLDCs is finding difficulty in performing even its most basic functions, with the basic services on which poor people often depend declining in quality and coverage.

Box 3.2 Child labour in India — and an Oxfam response

Children are the most obvious victims of poorly regulated labour markets. According to UNICEF, one in four children in the developing world is working. Despite the publicity in recent years concerning child labour in export industries, such as textiles and footwear, most child labour takes place in the household or on family land. In India, estimates of the number of child labourers vary widely, depending partly on age samples and definitions. But a figure of 80 million children of school age is probably realistic.[25] The majority of these children live in rural areas, reflecting high poverty levels and poor or non-existent education provision in village India. In India, there is also a close relationship between the labour status of women and the vulnerability of children. The social stigma attached to widowhood, and the limited labour-market opportunities of most widows, often leaves begging as the only survival strategy. The children of young widows are often forced by circumstance to supplement the household income.[26] Child labour is partly fostered by high levels of adult underemployment. If adults are able to command a fair price for their labour, there is less need for children to enter the labour market to supplement household incomes. Though household poverty and poor education provision are root causes of child labour, the phenomenon also depends on adults — either employers or parents — prepared to exploit children and benefit from their labour. There is a need for realistic responses to child labour, and many NGOs and governments are already working constructively towards giving children the opportunity to escape from their poverty.

In Bhavnagar City in Gujarat, India, Oxfam works with an Indian NGO providing alternative education for child labourers in the town's slums. The children work in a broad range of occupations, including home-based manufacturing, street vending, recycling, construction, and factory work. They face daily health and safety risks, and 15% of them report having been involved in serious workplace accidents. The project provides children with health and hygiene education, basic literacy in Gujarati, and numeracy skills. The latter two are especially important in protecting the children from being underpaid by employers and overcharged by sellers. The timetable accommodates normal working hours, and provides a savings scheme where children can safely deposit their earnings and learn basic money management. Projects such as these, which acknowledge the pressures that force children into the world of labour, can offer a window of hope to the next generation.

Gender in labour markets

Comparative advantage is dynamic, with economic development involving sectoral shifts as more capital-intensive technologies and new forms of labour specialisation are introduced. Development demands not only ongoing investment both in skills and infrastructure, but also changes in the way households and communities allocate time and resources. As has already been seen, where large numbers of people migrate to cities in search of prosperity and a better future for themselves and their children, major social changes follow. Those who remain in rural areas may only farm part-time, and increasingly supplement their incomes in the formal labour market. One salient feature of economic development is higher rates of female participation in labour markets, while children contribute less economically to the household as they stay longer in formal education. This presents both opportunities and problems for women, who tend to enjoy greater mobility in periods of rapid economic change, but who can also be squeezed by sectoral shifts and the failure of household divisions of labour to reflect the increased periods of time spent by women outside the household.

Women are also especially vulnerable to labour-market exploitation. Both in the developed and developing worlds, women's work is concentrated disproportionately in low-wage employment, and they are less likely than men to hold secure jobs. In China, the vulnerability of women to poverty and exploitation has been starkly illustrated during the economic changes of the past two decades. In particular, the costs of restructuring unprofitable state industries have been carried largely by women. In pre-reform China, women accounted for 38% of employees in state enterprises, yet since 1979 they have accounted for over 60% of redundancies. This has occurred in part because the government regards large numbers of unemployed men as a greater potential threat to social and political order than similar numbers of unemployed women. The results for many women have been devastating. Because social provision is based on residence and employment, and since no benefits scheme exists for the unemployed, laid-off workers depend on new work or employer compensation to avoid falls in income. Single women are especially vulnerable, and there has been a sharp rise in prostitution. In Guangdong province during a seven-month period in 1992 there were 25,000 arrests on charges of prostitution; migrant prostitution to Thailand has also witnessed a sharp rise.[27] Gender-biased and gender-blind policies often lead to counter-productive results, and equitable access for women to labour markets depends on governments regulating employers and, under some circumstances, creating incentives for fair employment conditions for women.

Rural livelihoods and poverty eradication

So far, this chapter has discussed livelihoods in the formal and informal sectors. Yet today, as 40 years ago, poverty is most severe and widespread among rural populations in the South. Generating equitable and rapid growth requires tackling the underlying causes of rural poverty, and making sustainable livelihoods a reality for the rural poor. Despite the 'urbanisation of poverty', from the Peruvian Altiplano to the plains of Northern India the most deprived and excluded sections of society continue to depend on the land for their survival. At least two thirds of the world's poor live in rural areas, and in some regions of the South rural poverty has proportionately increased. In East Asia especially, poverty has increasingly become a rural phenomenon, affecting farmers and agricultural wage-labourers who have not been reached by the new wealth of the last few decades of growth. In Indonesia, 70% of the population below the poverty line are smallholders and agricultural wage-labourers. In Thailand, where poverty is heavily concentrated in the isolated and rural north-east, 65% of the poor are renting land, or own very small areas of land. In South Asia and sub-Saharan Africa, where the population is predominantly rural and directly dependent on agriculture, poverty is overwhelmingly rural. In South Asia, at least 40 per cent of the rural population lives in absolute income poverty; in sub-Saharan Africa the proportion is more than 60 per cent. Even in Latin America, which is predominantly urban, rural poverty accounts for almost half of all income poverty. In Mexico, 55% of households below the poverty line depend on agriculture as the main source of income, and in Brazil, rural poverty rates are double those for urban areas, with half of the poor living in the countryside.

Where populations and markets are less concentrated, transaction costs — the hidden costs of participating in markets — are higher than in cities. But there are also specifically agricultural factors that help to account for the high incidence of rural poverty. It was noted earlier that labour-productivity rates in agriculture tend to be lower than those in other sectors. And while there are many people in rural areas who depend on fishing, logging, mining, manufacturing, and trading for their livelihoods, and a majority of rural households cannot be neatly fitted into any one occupational category, in most parts of the world agriculture remains the basis of the rural economy. Because of this fact, purchasing power tends to be lower and income-poverty higher in the countryside than in the city. There are underlying reasons for what has been described as the 'urban bias' in modern capitalist economies.[28] Six factors are identified here.

- The supply-side in most agricultural production is fragmented. Typically, there are many small-scale producers, and a handful of powerful intermediate firms controlling transport, storage, and marketing. Many agricultural producers are therefore vulnerable to monopsonies (markets in which there is only one buyer).

- Labour-efficiency gains in agriculture have the effect of reducing prices, and generating rural underemployment.

- There is a fairly inelastic demand for foodstuffs. This is known as 'Engel's law': as incomes rise, the proportion of its income that a society spends on food falls.

- The absence of effective cartels and price agreements for food commodities has led to volatile international market prices, making rural communities vulnerable to price collapses, as Table 3.4 shows.

- Monopsony-led consumer fashions in export markets — for example, for macadamia nuts or asparagus — can be short-lived and result in oversupply to export markets and price collapse.

- In agriculture there are delayed responses to price signals. For example, if prices fall for coffee, uprooting bushes which represent a long-term investment is usually not an option.

Land distribution, underemployment, and poverty

While there are structural reasons for rural poverty, a lack of access to land is often the most significant cause of poverty among rural populations. As Table 3.2 shows, where land distribution is especially uneven and landlessness is correspondingly high, underemployment and poverty follow. In part, this is because large farms, especially those growing commodities for export, tend to be capital-intensive and have relatively few backward linkages to firms in the domestic economy. Where landholding is concentrated, labour monopsonies also tend to result. Not only is the scope for selling one's labour to a highest bidder often limited or non-existent; the supply of rural, unskilled labour in the last three decades has seen a rapid absolute increase in most developing countries, despite the extent of urban migration. Rural wage rates have therefore been depressed and falling throughout Africa, Latin America, and South Asia since the mid-1970s. Alongside the increase in labour supply, increasing agricultural mechanisation has taken place — often as a response to antagonistic labour relations — significantly reducing demand. Finally, distorted land distribution also entails heavily unbalanced power relations which, from

Table 3.2 Unequal land distribution leads to high levels of rural poverty

(Sources: K. Griffin, *Alternative Strategies for Economic Development*, 1989; ILO, *World Employment 1995*; UNICEF, *State of the World's Children 1997*)

	GNP per capita US$ 000s 1994	Land ownership Gini Co-efficient	% of rural population in poverty 1980–89	% rural underemployed
Pakistan	430	0.61	29	—
Philippines	950	0.58	64	—
Brazil	2,970	0.85	34	—
Peru	2,110	0.95	83	75.9

Colombia to the Philippines, sustain a tradition of rural conflict, damaging rural production. Conflict perpetuates and creates poverty: infrastructure is destroyed, the most highly skilled people tend to migrate, long-term investments are rare in periods of uncertainty, there is restricted access to outside markets and important inputs, and male labour is often lost, only to be replaced by child labour and an increased burden on women.

Access to technology and rural poverty

One response to low levels of labour productivity and rural poverty has been to promote technological change as a substitute for institutional change. The green revolution of the 1960s, when High Yield Varieties (HYVs) of rice and wheat in particular were widely introduced in countries such as India, Mexico, Sri Lanka, and the Philippines, was motivated largely by a desire to avert a red revolution involving land reform. Numerous claims were made for the potential of HYVs to transform the rural economy, and in the early years of implementation the optimism appeared to be justified. The advantages of using HYVs as part of a coordinated rural development strategy were recognised by the Indonesian National Logistics Agency, Bulog, and this certainly contributed to the overall success of rural poverty-reduction initiatives in Indonesia. Farmers increased output massively, and not for the first time voices claimed that technology would single-handedly eradicate poverty.

Two particular advantages were identified by the proponents of the green revolution: first, that an increase in food supply would reduce prices, disproportionately benefiting the poor. Second, HYVs are equally effective whether used by smallholders or large commercial farms; in other words, they are 'scale-neutral'. The Philippines was the home of several strains of HYV rice, developed at the International Rice Research Institute, and almost 80% of rice area was sown with these HYVs by 1980. The effect on the rice crop and overall agricultural production was dramatic. The rice crop more than doubled during the period 1965–1982, from 4.1 million tons to 8.3 million tons. This increase was attributable almost entirely to the use of HYVs, rather than an increase in rice area or labour inputs. Between the mid-1970s and 1982, per capita agricultural production increased by almost 10%. Yet much of the optimism about the green revolution was to prove misplaced. Firstly, the impact has been extremely uneven, with irrigated farms in certain regions and sectors benefiting most. Lower food prices have benefited the urban poor, but since the rural poor are sellers of food, as well as buyers, their real purchasing power remained largely unchanged. Institutional biases, which the introduction of HYVs would supposedly circumvent, meant that large farmers were typically the first to innovate with HYVs, and to benefit from their use. The poorest farmers were the last to do so. Moreover, HYVs carry a much higher risk of crop failure than conventional strains, and optimal outcomes depend on the use of pesticides and fertilisers, most accessible to the wealthier farmers. Some of the gains from HYVs are offset by the cost of these additional inputs, which are themselves subject to price fluctuations, in turn leading to fluctuations in the agricultural surplus.

While in rural areas of the Philippines average per capita incomes have increased since the mid-1960s, overall rural poverty levels remain largely unchanged from the 1970s. Particularly hard hit have been the 1.2 million rural households dependent on corn sales. Oxfam works with corn farmers in rural Mindanao and the Cagayan valley, who are unable to compete with imports from more productive Thai and US farmers. Around 60 per cent of the total population in these areas is living below the World Bank's poverty line, and infant mortality rates are among the highest in the country. In general, the poorest and most isolated corn and rice farmers have been excluded from the market infrastructure and services that are needed if they are to escape from poverty. The root cause of the economic and political exclusion of the rural majority lies in the still unresolved issue of land distribution. Despite a recent rise in the land area under cultivation as a result of deforestation, the pace of population growth has meant that the average size of holding has fallen, to an average of 2.6 hectares, and the incidence of landlessness has increased. Given that two per cent of Filipino landowners control 36% of cultivated land, millions of households are scraping a living from plots well under the average hectarage. The Philippines holds an important lesson for other countries with highly unequal land distribution and high levels of poverty: the green revolution has proved to be insufficient by itself as a response to endemic rural poverty.

The case for land reform

While in some areas of the developing world, such as West Africa, it is still possible to expand smallholder farming output simply by bringing new land under cultivation, the Filipino case demonstrates that in most parts of the developing world a redistribution of land is crucial to rural poverty reduction. At the same time, land reform is not sufficient by itself as an anti-poverty measure. The quality of the land that is distributed, the presence of credit and infrastructural support, access to markets, and favourable prices all play a part in deciding the success of any land-reform programme. Land reform in Mexico, one of the great issues of the social revolution that began in 1910, failed to alleviate poverty in rural areas, because these associated measures were lacking. Peasants who worked the *ejidos*, or communal lands, remained mired in poverty. Yet there is overwhelming evidence from across the world that land reform, where carefully implemented, can have a dramatic impact on rural poverty levels and economic growth.[29]

In parts of Southern Africa and throughout Latin America, current patterns of rural landholding have their roots in colonial policy. In Zimbabwe, the most productive, higher-altitude land was the preserve of vast commercial estates under British rule in the 1920s. These farms, averaging 2,400 hectares in size and numbering about 4,700, remain overwhelmingly in the hands of white farmers and account for 80% of irrigated land. Access to credit is similarly unequal: together the commercial farms accounted for three quarters of the Agricultural Finance Corporation's lending in 1989-1990. Meanwhile, more than two million black farmers work mainly marginal communal areas, which suffer increasingly from degradation as households overwork the thin soil cover in an attempt to meet their most basic needs. The communal areas have no effective marketing system, a dearth of investment, and poor storage and transport infrastructure. Child malnutrition is endemic, both in communal areas and among the employees of commercial farms, whose labour is generally seasonal and underpaid. Thousands of men migrate to mining areas and towns in search of wage labour, causing profound social dislocation to many communities and often increasing the workload of women.

While the commercial agricultural sector is important in terms of foreign exchange — wheat, maize, *mange tout* peas, and flowers are destined mainly for European markets — it is heavily reliant on imported machinery and fertilisers and has few linkages to the domestic economy. It is also highly inefficient: no more than 40% of commercial farmland is under cultivation, suggesting that large-scale redistribution is possible without affecting current production. For decades, swathes of potentially highly productive land have lain unused, while thousands of Zimbabwean children have died from hunger-related disease. The current distribution of land in Zimbabwe and the poverty it perpetuates is also grossly inefficient: studies from across the developing world have consistently shown that small-scale farmers, when given access to credit and outside markets, make far more efficient use of land than do large commercial agribusinesses. Not only is there often an *inverse* relationship between farm size and productivity, small farms are also more labour-intensive than large farms, having an equalising effect on incomes. Yet despite this, the pace of land reform in Zimbabwe since independence in 1980 has been sluggish: initial plans for resettlement have been all but abandoned after just 50,000 families were resettled. A well organised challenge to the Land Acquisition Act in 1992 by commercial farmers meant that by 1995 the government had bought only 21 of the designated farms. More recently, the government has proposed a piecemeal land-reform programme, under an 'indigenisation' drive designed to end the economic dominance of white Zimbabweans. However, the few farms that have been 'redistributed' to date have been handed out as political favours, rather than as part of a coherent poverty reduction strategy. For the foreseeable future, meaningful change in the distribution of land and the living conditions of Zimbabwe's rural poor remains unlikely.[30]

Land reform and poverty reduction: Taiwan and South Korea

The political difficulties of land redistribution are often cited as an argument against land reform. Ironically, it was precisely to counter the appeal of communism among the rural poor that land reform was undertaken in Taiwan and South Korea during the 1950s, radically altering the distribution of assets, and building the basis for rapid and equitable economic growth during later decades. The dramatic reduction in the incidence of poverty in South Korea and Taiwan has been closely related to their success in transferring surplus rural labour supply into the growing urban industrial and services sectors, while at the same time achieving significant productivity gains in small-scale agriculture.

When the Japanese colonial occupation of Taiwan ended in 1945, the wealthiest two per cent of landowners owned 33 per cent of the land, while 40 per cent of agricultural households survived on less than ten per cent of the total. Almost half of all households were completely landless. Between the arrival of the Kuomintang on the island in 1949, and 1953, land was redistributed on a huge scale, estimated at a value equivalent to 13% of GNP: one quarter of all cultivated land was parcelled out to the poorest 48% of agricultural households. By 1960, fewer than 15 per cent of all agricultural households subsisted as tenant farmers. The landlord class virtually ceased to exist, their share of farming income falling from 25% to just 6%. In less than a decade, the Taiwanese countryside was transformed: the rural population played a major part in implementing the reforms, and, once they were completed, in the day-to-day running of local economic affairs. The provision of good-quality education created a class of competent smallholders capable of efficient administration of their own affairs. Farmers' associations provided credit and marketing networks and crop-storage facilities, set up processing plants, and managed local irrigation systems. Participative structures worked so well because there was a high degree of asset equality; there was limited scope for the associations to be exploited by powerful minority interests; and every farmer had an interest in ensuring the success of local projects.[31]

In South Korea, Japanese colonialism had left a legacy of smallholder agriculture, with good irrigation and infrastructural support. Post-war land reform completed this process, with limits placed on the area of paddy that any one household could own. At the same time, rice imports were prohibited, with subsidies for the urban consumer and generous fixed prices for farmers. The small size of the average farm has contributed to an increase in part-time farming in recent years: close to one third of farming households now earn less than half of their income from agriculture — and an increase in productivity as plots have been farmed intensively. Over the last two decades, real value-added per farmer has risen by an annual average of 6.4%. Fertiliser and pesticide use, together with the use of high-yield strains, has been behind this dramatic increase in productivity.[32] Rural asset-equality was the springboard for advances in other areas of the economy: the land-reform experiences of these two NICs are closely connected to their success in export-led industrialisation, relative political stability, and poverty reduction. One danger of land reform, cited by its opponents, is that it can return agriculture to a subsistence base. But, as Taiwan and South Korea demonstrate, there is no necessary conflict between asset equality and rapid growth.

Rural credit and poverty reduction

The rural poor are widely denied access to formal credit and banking facilities, and this, along with access to land and basic social provision, is a key obstacle to the ability of people in rural areas to secure a viable livelihood. Unfavourable geography, illiteracy, and a lack of collateral leave many of the rural poor vulnerable to informal credit arrangements through local landlords or full-time money lenders, often involving punitive interest rates. Elsewhere, poor communities may arrange their own informal savings and lending schemes. The potential benefits of reliable and stable savings and investment facilities for poor communities and households are considerable. Savings function as a form of insurance during lean periods caused by drought, illness, and unemployment, and can cushion the effects of falls in income or rises in costs. Credit can promote growth and bring long-term benefits to the rural poor, and may be needed for a number of reasons: to purchase assets, or as working capital, for health expenditure, custom and ritual, or school fees, or for repayment of previous debts. Poor people are rarely familiar with banking procedure, and can save and borrow only small sums; commercial banks are usually unwilling to provide for them. Easy access — in terms of minimal bureaucracy, proximity, and easily available loans — is important for poor rural users, as are low interest and a waiver on collateral.

The potential benefits of accessible savings and credit facilities for the rural poor have long been recognised, and policy failures among state-owned rural development banks have led in recent years to microfinance and rural credit being viewed as an area in which NGOs enjoy a comparative advantage. Whereas state banks such as IRDP in India were characterised by a lack of coherence, poor targeting, exploitation by political interests, and a lack of impact on rural poverty,[33] NGO banks have been celebrated for their capacity to target poor households, and their flexibility and responsiveness to local needs. The result has been an explosion in the numbers of small and medium-scale credit and savings facilities being established by NGOs. The Grameen and BRAC schemes in Bangladesh are perhaps the best-known of the NGO credit-delivery systems, and together they have more than 1.5 million users, most of whom are women. Most notable about these schemes are their repayment rates of over 90%, demonstrating the feasibility of efficient microfinance schemes.

Box 3.3 Two Oxfam-supported credit schemes

In Queretaro in central Mexico, Oxfam works with a partner providing credit to poor rural households. The Union Regional de Apoyo Campesino has 5,000 members in 27 villages in an area with high levels of male out-migration to the USA and Mexican cities, high rates of seasonal unemployment, and poorly developed infrastructure. The farmers were hit particularly hard by the 1994 *peso* crisis and subsequent inflation. The bank mobilises local savings, maintaining a high level of internally generated funds, and only savers are entitled to borrow, which creates a sense of collective ownership. The balance must be 20% of loan size, but otherwise there is easy access and few regulations: URAC allows its members to save as much or as little as they choose with a village cashier, while withdrawals must be made at a central URAC office. Interest is broadly in line with commercial rates. It has proved to be an important form of security for villagers: withdrawals are made in particular during periods of high expenditure, such as childbirth and religious festivals, and accounts are available with fixed withdrawal dates, such as when a baby is due. Users have cited consumption during periods of unemployment, clothing, school fees (which are increased if payments are late), and medical bills as reasons for withdrawal.[34]

Credit facilities need not necessarily provide financial services, and in areas with a recent history of hyperinflation, long-term saving in another commodity may offer greater security. Another Oxfam partner, the Kebkabiya Smallholders' Charitable Society in North Darfur, Sudan, runs a community-based seed-bank scheme as part of a rural development programme. The scheme covers 65,000 villagers in 120 villages dependent on the thin, sandy, rain-fed soils of the region. Droughts are a regular occurrence in Darfur, and food security is a major issue for villagers. After the 1984-1985 famine in the area, Oxfam decided to establish seed-banks, which operate much like an ordinary bank. The bank is stocked with seed purchased from a revolving fund. Once the capital investment brings a dividend, the loan is repaid with ten per cent interest (ten *kora*, or measuring bowls of seed, are repaid with eleven after harvest). In time a community reserve is created, for use in drought years. If the surplus becomes too large to be stored, some of it can be sold for cash, and the money distributed proportionately among savers or used for maintaining the banks. Earlier experience in a similar project in Sudan forced Oxfam to reassess its approach and promote community-based participation in the banks. Previously, Oxfam had constructed and stocked the banks itself, and in an area with a long history of aid interventions during drought periods, villagers assumed that this was another handout. Seed was not repaid, and villagers told fieldworkers that they were waiting for the government to come and replenish the stocks. In Kebkabiya, the villagers built the banks themselves, using local materials. Once the loans were explained and villagers understood that repayment affected everyone's long-term security, repayment levels were high enough to build up a substantial stock, and in time a central bank for the area, further spreading risk. 'Social collateral' reduced lending risk, with village seed-bank committees putting pressure on defaulters, and repayment couched in terms of obligation to fellow villagers.[35]

Both the URAC and Kebkabiya schemes demonstrate how, under the right conditions, poor people can be reliable savers and efficient investors, improving their standard of living and strengthening a cycle of rising productivity.

The limitations of credit

However, even where credit schemes are effectively targeted and administered, they have limitations. The most obvious problem is that, in order to invest, one needs something to invest in, and for assetless people credit is of limited use. Reaching the very poorest through credit schemes may therefore be a misplaced objective, though investment by wealthier villagers may have community-wide benefits, for example by generating employment opportunities. Certainly, there is evidence that the very poorest are widely excluded from microfinance schemes, and families with the highest initial income levels have the highest levels of asset retention and loan repayment. In the case of the URAC scheme (see Box 3.3), those who were heavily indebted to moneylenders and local landlords at the time of the scheme's introduction were in no position to save, and therefore were excluded; as were those who exhausted their savings after becoming ill or permanently injured. These people were left with few prospects of escaping from extreme poverty, and remained vulnerable to exploitation by moneylenders offering untied credit.

Another problem is that the poor are generally unskilled, and therefore restricted in their range of income-earning opportunities, with or without access to credit. This is a particular problem in parts of South Asia where a caste-based division of labour applies, and scheduled castes are confined to quickly saturated sections of the labour and product market, such as barber's shops and leatherwork. Ensuring that users control loans once they gain access to them is an additional problem. Many development writers have cited targeted lending to women by Bangladeshi NGO banks as a positive example of women's economic and social empowerment through micro-level NGO interventions. Yet, while there is evidence of women's status being enhanced by their access to a source of revenue, appropriation by men of women's loans — for which women assume repayment responsibility — is a significant problem.[36]

Finally, there is a problem of sustainability and financial independence. Here especially NGO advantages are exaggerated, with claims of superiority based more on state failure than on adequately analysed NGO success. Many microfinance schemes continue to depend on external support and subsidised interest rates, in order to attract target groups. There is continuing debate about whether social collateral can remain effective over long periods of time as a mechanism for reducing risk, and what sort of participatory measures do and don't work in terms of promoting both financial viability and poverty reduction. It cannot be assumed either that the history of state involvement in rural credit provision is one of straightforward failure, or that the NGO experience is an unqualified success. NGO interventions have sometimes taken place where they have not been best placed to provide financial services for the poor, while during the late 1980s Indonesia's Bank Rakyat (BRI), a state-owned commercial bank, made a significant contribution to rural economic growth and poverty reduction, effectively targeting rural smallholders below the poverty line.[37]

A case for a rural development strategy

All the factors identified in this section – high transaction costs and structural factors, unequal access to land and technology, and weakly developed credit markets — conspire to prevent rural development keeping apace of urban development. In addition, classic models of development have tended to neglect the issue of rural development, focusing instead on the building of industrial capacity. Yet markets for agriculture in particular often have to be developed. This often involves substantial costs, some of which need to be met by an activist state.[38] Despite the need for state-supported rural development strategies, in many developing countries there has been a general under-capitalisation of rural areas. This has applied both to investment in smallholder farming and to physical and communications infrastructure, and the results have been profoundly disequalising.[39] Yet rural development is realisable, and some OECD countries — such as Denmark and New Zealand — with favourable climates and land-labour ratios have successfully pursued an agricultural path to development. Nonetheless, rural development requires strategies that recognise urban bias, and the need to improve productivity and terms of trade for farmers.

Reaching the very poorest in rural areas through public-policy interventions is not as straightforward as it might appear at first. The problems of 'leakage', discussed briefly in the opening chapter, often mean that correcting the urban bias has disequalising effects in rural areas. For example, the benefits of fixed prices for agricultural producers are captured disproportionately by those producers with the largest surpluses; and fertiliser subsidies similarly direct gains towards larger and more prosperous farmers. This is not a necessary reason *not* to intervene in rural markets, but it does highlight the importance of exercising caution in rural development policy. Of course, the more equal the system of land-owning, the fewer the distortions: Indonesia's broadly successful rural development strategy was grounded in extremely equitable land distribution, whereas the state-subsidised Banco Agrario in Peru, prior to its abolition, functioned largely as a source of subsidy to the wealthier strata of rural society. Although there is no magic formula that will resolve the structural causes of rural poverty, institutional failures can be identified which have unnecessarily exacerbated the marginalisation of many rural populations. These institutional failures, most notably a lack of access to land, credit markets, technology, social provision, and the sources of political power, are mutually reinforcing, and intensify economic and social exclusion in the countryside.

Rural development strategies which resolve these institutional biases and reduce poverty in the countryside are crucial to equitable and sustained growth. A two-tier pattern of growth will result otherwise, with an enclave 'peri-urban' economy leading to growing disparities between rural and urban areas. This has happened in Peru, where economic growth since 1993 has had a negligible impact on rural poverty. The sudden insertion of the protected rural economy into competitive commodity and labour markets has further weakened the capacity of farming households to secure a livelihood. In such instances, policies that strengthen the rural supply response to global competition are needed.

Of course, rural development cannot meaningfully be viewed in isolation from urban development. Agricultural growth has a strong effect on growth in predominantly urban sectors of the economy; each 1%

of growth in agriculture leads to 1.5% of growth in manufacturing, construction, and services.[40] Conversely, patterns of urban development affect how the countryside develops. The city provides valuable income-earning opportunities for many rural households and is a major market for farmers. Meanwhile, rural development programmes can benefit urban areas, relieving infrastructural pressures on cities by stemming migration and the rural–urban transfer of poverty. In the Indian state of West Bengal, the state government has had considerable success in slowing migration to the already overcrowded city of Calcutta by pursuing land reform, rural credit, and physical-infrastructure and clean-water programmes in rural areas. Integrating rural and urban development strategies, and understanding the linkages between livelihood opportunities in the city and the countryside, is vital to the success of poverty-eradication goals.

Globalisation: new pressures on livelihoods

Globalisation became one of the buzz-words of the 1990s. It refers to a set of disparate trends in global trade and investment and culture over the last decade. With the end of the Cold War, the insertion of China – with one fifth of the world's population — into the global economy, the rapid export-based growth of the East Asian economies until 1997, the growth in regional trade agreements, and the introduction of a new global trade and investment regime with the conclusion of the Uruguay Round of the General Agreement on Tariffs and Trade (GATT),[41] the world is a more integrated place than ever before. In particular, globalisation raises fundamental questions about the future role of the state in economic and social development. Is the state's role to protect the most vulnerable from the chill winds of global competition, to facilitate the rapid and irreversible expansion of markets, or to reform the status quo in favour of the poor? Our answers to the questions that globalisation poses carry profound implications for the future shape of economic and social relations between and within societies.

Some commentators have argued that the effects of globalisation are exaggerated, noting that in many ways the world is no more integrated today than at the end of the last century. For example, trade accounts for a proportion of global GDP today similar to that in the nineteenth-century heyday of British-dominated 'free trade'. But, while true, this observation misses the point: the character of integration today differs fundamentally from that a century ago. Communications, shipping, and travel are massively cheaper than they were two generations ago. Financial markets have grown exponentially in recent years, with Foreign Direct Investment (FDI) flows increasing sixfold between 1985 and 1995, and fourfold since 1990.[42] As the East Asian financial crisis illustrates, change has been most fundamental, and influential in terms of implications for poverty eradication, in foreign-exchange markets, where turnover has increased more than a thousandfold since 1970. In 1996, the *daily* turnover of foreign-exchange markets exceeded $1.2 trillion, roughly equivalent to the Gross National Product of France, the world's fourth largest economy. The ability of governments, especially in developing countries, to control the spread of financial crises is limited under the current global system. As Box 3.4 illustrates, new technology is also radically changing the nature of direct investments.

Box 3.4 Foreign direct investment (FDI) and new technologies: a changing picture

Historically, FDI flows in developing countries have been directed principally to foodstuffs and minerals, called primary commodities, and low- and medium-technology manufactures. But high technology is increasingly challenging the high-tech/high-productivity/high-wage correlation in key global industries. For example, in Bangalore in Southern India, software engineers in the city's fast-growing microchip industry are paid one tenth of Silicon Valley wages, by US firms which have relocated parts of their operations in order to exploit high human-capital levels, allied to low labour costs, among educated Indians.[43] And in Hermosillo in Mexico, a Ford plant built in 1986, which unlike the company's other Mexican plants uses Just-In-Time and Total Quality Control procedures, achieves higher quality levels than any of Ford's North American plants, similar productivity rates to those of US workers, and has a markedly smaller wage bill.[44] While Mexican worker productivity rose from one fifth to one third of the US level between 1989 and 1993, Mexican labour continues to cost one sixth of US labour. This ready availability and mobility of high technology is already contributing to a downward pressure on wage levels among semi- and low-skilled workers in the North and the South.

The implications of globalisation

What are the implications of these developments for poverty eradication and inequality, and what sorts of pressure is globalisation placing on livelihoods both in the industrial and developing countries? According to proponents of free trade, trade and investment liberalisation creates a win-win situation. Poor countries which open their economies will receive a flood of foreign investment, generating badly needed jobs, developing human and physical capital stocks, and transferring valuable technologies. The advanced countries, meanwhile, stand to gain from new cheap labour sources, growing competition, and vast new markets for their products. John F. Kennedy was fond of describing the US economy as a rising tide of prosperity lifting all the boats on the water. This same optimism has driven the liberalising efforts of the IMF and many industrial-country governments. Of course, the logic of the free market is not applied uniformly. While protectionist trade and investment policies are swept aside, movements of unskilled labour are more tightly regulated than at any point in history. And, as the Uruguay Round demonstrated, both the USA and the European Union are uninterested in meaningful liberalisation of heavily subsidised 'sensitive' agricultural products.

Meanwhile, the more extreme opponents of liberalisation present the new competitive pressures associated with globalisation as a downward spiral into environmental degradation and exploitation of labour. In reality, the costs and benefits are more mixed, and globalisation is producing both winners and losers. While growing market integration and growth in trade, FDI, and financial flows over the last decade have offered some developing countries new opportunities to develop competitive advantages, the terms of the Uruguay Round actually reinforced the economic marginalisation of the Least Developed Countries. Sub-Saharan Africa, where the majority of Least Developed Countries are located, stands to lose more than $1 billion a year as a result of the Uruguay Round terms.[45] Foreign-exchange losses worth $1 billion translate into falling incomes, less secure livelihoods, a growing dependence on aid at a time when aid flows are shrinking, government revenues foregone, and further obstacles to desperately needed improvements in health and education. The risk is that sub-Saharan Africa will be permanently relegated to the status of economic laggard, at a time when the region is in desperate need of trade and investment opportunities which could

121

offer a route out of poverty. Over the period 1980–1995, the value of the region's merchandise exports actually *fell* from $51bn to $45bn, while those of Latin America more than doubled, East Asia's increased fivefold, and South Asia's, albeit from a very low base, more than tripled. The region as a whole averaged GDP growth of little more than two per cent a year during this period, with per capita GDP declining in real terms by more than ten per cent.[46]

Under the new trade and investment regime, benefits have been distributed extremely unevenly, not least because the rules reflect the priorities of the economically powerful rather than the needs of the poor. While the World Trade Organisation (WTO), created out of the Uruguay Round Trade talks, provides a valuable forum for arbitration in trade disputes, few developing countries have the technical and financial resources to participate effectively in the WTO and ensure that their interests are represented. The WTO has so far largely failed to provide a 'level playing field' in trade relations between countries in the North and South, at a time when the terms of trade for the majority of the poorest countries continue to deteriorate.

The share in global trade of the low-income countries has steadily fallen over the last two decades to barely one third of its 1980 level.[47] And, as Table 3.3 shows, direct investment in developing countries has been concentrated in a handful of major emerging economies in Latin America and Asia, reinforcing existing regional inequalities. The growth in FDI has undoubtedly generated employment, with the ILO claiming that 12 million jobs were created directly in developing countries as a result of FDI in the first half of the decade.[48] Yet because of the concentration of FDI flows, those countries in the South worst hit by the depression of the 1980s have not benefited significantly in employment terms. Contrary to some of the more extravagant claims made for trade and investment liberalisation, the expansion of FDI has not rescued workforces who were laid off or saw their real incomes fall during the 'lost decade' in Latin American and African countries. In these regions especially, FDI has been concentrated in capital-intensive primary-commodity industries with limited direct effects on employment. Because FDI in primary commodities tends also to involve few 'backward linkages' to suppliers in the domestic economy, the net effect on livelihoods in the wider economy is also small.[49]

Table 3.3 Net FDI to developing countries and regions

(Source: World Bank, *World Development Indicators 1997)*

	Billions of US$		As % of GNP
	1991–1993	**1994–1996**	**1990–1996** average
Developing-country total	**144.3**	**288.7**	**1.3**
East Asia and Pacific	**71.7**	**157.0**	**3.3**
of which			
China	43.1	111.9	—
Malaysia	14.2	16.3	—
Indonesia	5.3	12.2	—
Thailand	5.9	6.4	—
Latin America and Caribbean	**39.3**	**73.0**	**1.3**
of which			
Mexico	13.5	24.4	—
Brazil	4.5	13.5	—
Argentina	8.5	3.9	—
Chile	2.0	5.7	—
Sub-Saharan Africa	**4.0**	**7.9**	**2.2**
South Asia	**1.9**	**5.6**	**0.2**
Middle East and North Africa	**8.2**	**4.9**	**0.5**
Low income, excluding China	9.9	18.3	0.7
Middle income	91.3	158.5	1.0

Globalisation, wages, and labour standards

Not only have global trade and investment patterns made a limited impact in terms of generating new livelihood opportunities where they are most needed, in many situations these trends have created poverty and generated inequalities, placing new pressures on livelihoods. According to liberal economic orthodoxy, liberalisation should have led to an upsurge in demand for unskilled labour, reducing poverty levels and inequalities. Yet in even the most enthusiastic liberalisers, this has not happened.[50] In both Latin America and East Asia, income inequalities have increased markedly in the wake of liberalisation, and in Latin America the modest economic recovery of the last few years has had little impact on the living standards of the poor. At the same time, inequalities in incomes and health status are growing in many developed economies, with a small number of people capturing most of the benefits of economic growth.

There are vigorous debates about the causes of these recent and rising inequalities between regions and within countries. One major factor appears to be that the rate of increase in demand for unskilled labour has been outstripped by the rate of increase in its supply; and oversupply lowers prices. At the same time, labour-productivity increases among semi-skilled and low-skilled workers in the industrialised countries have in most cases stagnated since the 1970s. This means that wages have too; and in order to protect their standard of living, women have entered formal labour markets in increasing numbers. This trend has increased the numbers of unskilled adults seeking employment, adding further downward pressure on wages.[51]

Simultaneously, globalisation has made low-wage labour pools in poor countries more accessible as investment controls have been relaxed. Industrialised-country manufacturers and, increasingly, service-sector firms are able to outsource work to poor countries, with the effect of weakening the bargaining power of organised labour in both the North and South. The supply of unskilled and semi-skilled labour of the sort needed for assembly work or data processing is almost limitless. This oversupply of unskilled labour has facilitated a shift in the balance of power between workers and capital, with growing repression of organised labour justified by governments and employers on the dubious grounds that, in the new globally competitive climate, labour rights constitute a competitive disadvantage.

With stagnating productivity and wages among less skilled workers, profits have risen relative to wage income. However, the minority of people able to respond to the new market opportunities presented by globalisation have reaped considerable benefits. Growing competition in the wake of liberalisation has generated a growth in innovation and new technologies, as firms seek to capture markets in industries with high added value. This technological change has led to a rapid increase in the demand for specialisation and particular skills, discussed in Chapter 2. In contrast to unskilled and semi-skilled labour, the skills needed in most fast-growing high-value industries are in short supply. As a consequence, the wages of certain skill-intensive sectors have risen extremely rapidly, leading to gaping inequalities in wealth. Whereas in 1960 the income-share ratio of the richest fifth and the poorest fifth of the world's population stood at 30:1, today it stands at 78:1. The world's seven richest countries in per capita terms have an average income 39 times higher than the seven poorest countries, a figure that is up from 20 in 1960. Within countries, both in the North and the South, income disparities have widened.[52] These widening inequalities require extremely urgent responses, since they impede poverty reduction — as the discussion of the poverty-reduction elasticity of growth in the first chapter showed — and inhibit growth. Global growth rates are 2% slower than in capitalism's post-war 'golden age', and are proving less effective in reducing poverty. According to the UN Conference on Trade and Development, financial liberalisation has made the trading of existing assets more profitable than direct investment, with profound consequences for the poor. Less employment and investment is being generated by profits than was the case 30 years ago, and equity has consequently suffered.[53]

Box 3.5 Globalisation and the experience of Latin America

In Latin America, trade and investment liberalisation has been pursued with an unusual fervour by governments over the past decade. The results have not been encouraging. Growth has remained uneven, income inequalities have generally worsened, with little of the new wealth reaching those in greatest need, and poverty and violence continue to characterise daily life for tens of millions of people. The detrimental impact of trade and investment liberalisation on the livelihoods of the poor has been exacerbated by a number of regional factors. The first is the gross inequality in educational access and outcomes and the shortage of skilled labour, discussed in the previous section, and the impact this has had on wage levels in non-tradable sectors. A second factor is the types of goods exported from Latin America. Primary commodities account for one third of the region's exports, and these primary industries create fewer jobs than does labour-intensive manufacturing. Finally, extensive labour-market deregulation, particularly in Chile and Mexico, which coincided with liberalisation, weakened the power of organised labour. Liberalisation carries high transition costs, and many Latin American countries were unduly hasty in deregulating markets and exposing their populations to international competition. The IMF and World Bank, along with free-trade proponents in Latin American governments, feared that a sequenced transition would stall, and that the only way of guaranteeing the full insertion of markets into the global economy was an irreversible 'shock' liberalisation.

One effect of rapid liberalisation, rather than a sequenced liberalisation programme which would have given more firms time to adjust, was that many previously protected labour-intensive manufacturing firms were uncompetitive in global markets. Manufacturing in most of Latin America has been in marked decline as a proportion of GDP since liberalisation began (see Figure 3.1). In Brazil, one million manufacturing jobs have been lost in the last eight years, as the proportion of the workforce in manufacturing fell from 22% to 18%. This may represent a return to natural comparative advantage under freer trade conditions, yet it has also caused an increase in underemployment and open unemployment, with the services sector already saturated.[54] This has been a pattern repeated across Latin America. The poor paid a high price, in terms of lost livelihoods and new social pressures, for the hasty insertion of their economies into global markets. In Mexico, financial liberalisation led directly to the *peso* crisis, in the wake of which the domestic economy imploded, with the majority of Mexican medium-sized firms going bankrupt. Today, Mexico has one of the most malnourished populations in Latin America, with two thirds of Mexicans underfed. Safety nets for the poor are non-existent in some areas, and insufficient in others, while social funds such as PRONASOL, which were intended to improve social provision for the poor, were used instead as tools of political patronage, buying votes for the ruling party, and failed to target the poorest communities.[55] Across the region, the capacity of the poor to respond to new competitive challenges was limited further by limited physical infrastructure, poor credit access as banks reduced their loan-to-deposit ratios during stabilisation periods, weak investment incentives for the poor, and poor education and training systems. Today, wealth in Latin America is more unequally distributed than ever before, poverty remains the reality for 200 million people, and rapid growth remains elusive.

Rural livelihoods and global linkages: commodity trade

In terms of poverty reduction, globalisation threatens to become a lost opportunity. Instead of developing trade and investment regimes which serve the interests and needs of the poorest countries, a system has been developed where those societies in greatest need of growth and recovery stand to gain least. Not only have increased investment and trade benefited a minority of mostly middle-income countries: the Least Developed Countries have also been squeezed in primary-commodity production, their principal area of natural comparative advantage. Declining and volatile prices over the last 20 years have had often disastrous consequences for rural communities who depend for their livelihoods on growing cash crops for export. The poorest countries depend overwhelmingly on unprocessed foodstuffs, fibres, and minerals for their foreign exchange. Of sub-Saharan Africa's total merchandise export figure in 1993, about one third, or $13bn, was in non-fuel primary commodities, with many countries dependent on only one or two primary commodities for upwards of 80% of their export earnings.[56] These unstable and falling prices have been central factors in persistently high rates of rural poverty.

The effect has been twofold. First, the impact on current-account deficits of falling commodity prices, allied to stagnant demand, has been a major factor in the development of the debt crisis in developing countries. After a round of reckless lending to and borrowing by developing-country governments in the late 1970s, interest-rate rises in the early 1980s tripled repayment costs. These debts had to be repaid in foreign exchange — which depended on export earnings. These export earnings were falling precipitously, however. It is estimated that in 1992 alone a staggering $65bn was lost to commodity-exporting developing economies as a result of trends in unit prices. This sum is seven billion dollars *more* than the total official aid budget of OECD members in that year.[57] IMF adjustment programmes that insisted on export-promotion measures, including currency depreciation, as a condition of financial support compounded the situation for a number of developing countries. Cocoa is a case in point: several producers were simultaneously encouraged to promote cocoa exports, with the result that in West Africa production increased from 1.6 to 2.3 million tons over the 1980s, while prices more than halved from $2.6 to $1.2 per kilogram.

Increasingly onerous debt repayments in LLDCs have contributed to a rapid decline in public spending on the basics that are valued by poor rural communities — schools, health clinics, roads, electricity, and clean water — while the laws of political expediency mean that rural communities tend to be worst affected by falling public expenditure. The result is deepening poverty in rural areas, and widening inequalities within countries in the South.

Table 3.4 Commodity prices, 1980–1995 *(Source:* UNCTAD 1995; World Bank, *World Development Indicators 1997)*

Commodity price index	1980	1985	1991	1992	1993	1994	1995
Non-fuel commodities	**174**	**133**	**93**	**86**	**86**	**101**	**102**
Agriculture	191	145	96	88	93	112	110
Metals and minerals	132	102	87	81	70	77	85
Food	191	124	97	92	104	114	113
Beverages (cents/kg) 1990 $							
Cocoa	361.6	328.6	116.9	103.2	105.1	126.7	120.0
Coffee, robustas	450.4	386.1	104.9	88.2	108.9	237.8	232.1
Coffee, other milds	481.4	471.0	183.3	132.4	146.8	300.2	279.1

Second, the decline in terms of trade for non-fuel commodities has had a direct effect on government revenues independently of the debt crisis, and on the ability of poor producer households to meet their basic needs. The money generated from growing cash crops for export allows poor households to pay for school fees, transport, fuel, and clothing. A decline in income directly affects welfare.

The implications of the commodity crisis extend beyond the countries of the South, however. In the Andean countries of South America, the consequences of commodity-price volatility and decline have been felt farther afield on the streets of cities in the industrialised countries. Farmers unable to secure a viable income from licit crops such as cocoa and anatto turned in their thousands during the 1980s to growing coca, the plant used in the production of cocaine and crack-cocaine, for Colombian drug cartels.

Despite the urgent need for diversification and price stability for the poorest countries, the World Trade Organisation has singularly failed to address the issues of pricing and dependence. Clearly, promoting sustainable rural livelihoods demands a policy response at a number of levels. Equitable access to land, to credit and technology, and to good-quality social provisioning that is relevant to the needs of rural communities is an essential component of any strategy designed to achieve equitable growth. But so is international action on commodity pricing and debt. UNCTAD's Integrated Programme for Commodities — with its stated aim of improving terms of trade for producers, stabilising prices, and encouraging local processing, where much of the added value lies — points the way forward in resolving some of the structural imbalances from which rural producers suffer.

The scope for reform

What is the right response to the failure of globalisation to deliver development to a large proportion of the developing world's population? However unequally gains and losses are being distributed under the current rules, returning to the protectionism of the post-war years is not a viable or desirable route to development. Globalisation need not be a zero-sum game, with some people and countries winning at the expense of others. The right way forward is to reform the rules, enabling poor people to identify and respond to globalisation's opportunities, and to participate in new markets on more equitable terms.

In all of this, basic rights and social objectives are not negotiable. At the national level, workers who are displaced by competition should be retrained and reintegrated into labour markets; especially vulnerable groups need labour-market protection; and the disenfranchised must be given a political voice if their rights are not to be trampled. This means giving the poorest an economic stake, through redistributive policies and access to good-quality social provision. Liberalisation must be managed carefully and applied selectively by developing countries. Infant industries may need protection over the medium term; FDI in strategic industries may need to be controlled; and short-term capital flows should be limited in immature financial markets. At the international level, poverty eradication must be adopted as the explicit priority of the international community. At present, the scramble for prizes from liberalisation has ignored concerns about poverty, with growth often being promoted as if it is an end in itself. Reform of trade regimes that place the poorest countries at a disadvantage is also an urgent necessity. 'Anti-deficit radicalism', where the onus for controls on inflation is placed on individual countries in deficit, and the costs of deflationary policies are borne largely by the poor, is inimical to poverty eradication and is undermining long-term development efforts. Stable sources of liquidity for poor countries, a transaction tax on short-term capital flows, and a larger lender of last resort, better suited than the IMF to the task of meeting the needs of developing countries, are all crucial reforms.

Finally, international action to stop a 'race to the bottom' in labour and environmental standards is needed. Part of this strategy is to strengthen the core conventions of the International Labour Organisation; while another important component is for obligations to be placed on individual investors in the form of 'codes of conduct'. The list of proposals made here for reform constitutes only a broad overview, and does not aim to be comprehensive. The need for reform to the current trade and investment regimes, and a more gradual insertion of the developing countries into global markets, is clear, however. The risk is that the potential for development will be lost unless the opportunities presented by globalisation are distributed more widely and more justly. Perhaps the most important lesson to draw from current poverty trends is that the right to a viable livelihood can be realised only under conditions of relative equality. For these conditions to be created, and for markets to operate fairly and efficiently, an accountable state is needed to operate a system of regulations and incentives favouring broad-based growth.

Box 3.6 Universal respect for labour rights[58]

Globalisation has brought with it a recognition on the part of governments that integrated global capital and product markets demand a regulatory framework if they are to function efficiently. The World Trade Organisation, though inadequate, is a regulatory response to these changing international conditions. Yet a regulatory framework to protect basic labour standards has been notably absent from the trade and investment agenda. The development of a social clause, helping to bring about a more equitable distribution of the benefits of trade and foreign investment, could help to fill this gap. The opponents of a social clause have pointed out the proposal's limitations, noting that its impact would be felt principally in the export sector. It is argued that poverty and exploitation would be displaced rather than eradicated.

Certainly, exaggerated claims have sometimes been made for the potential impact of a social clause. It is also the case that unless the causes of poverty — exclusion from assets, political power, and markets — are resolved, problems arising from the denial of labour rights, child labour, rural underemployment, and labour-market discrimination are unlikely to be resolved. However, abuse of basic rights should not be tolerated as a source of competitive advantage, and institutionalised abuses of labour rights, by no means confined to developing countries, might be covered by some form of sanction. Oxfam is part of a growing international consensus in favour of the enforcement of basic labour rights, and campaigns for a number of strategies at national and international levels to protect the basic rights of workers.[59] A basic ILO social clause could function, in much the same way as the Universal Declaration of Human Rights does, as an authoritative point of reference for the raising of standards. It could also directly protect a significant number of workers in export industries who are currently denied basic rights. The ILO and WTO could jointly administer such a social clause. The ILO is best placed to monitor compliance and judge infringements, given that the framework for monitoring standards already largely exists. Moreover, the ILO's tripartite structure lends it legitimacy, assuming as it does the freedom of employer–employee association. The World Trade Organisation would provide enforcement through its dispute-settlement mechanism.

Oxfam also supports strengthening the supervisory mechanisms that regulate the ILO 'core conventions', which have themselves informed and been informed by the Universal Declaration of Human Rights. Oxfam believes that ILO Conventions 87 and 98, on the right to freedom of association and the right to collective bargaining, are the best starting points. Once these basic principles are enshrined in a new social clause, it would provide a good basis for improving observance of labour rights. These two conventions must be accepted as non-negotiable and universally binding. The right to a livelihood cannot be isolated from other rights, and development strategies based on exploited labour will fail.

Livelihoods: policy guidelines for equity, poverty reduction, and growth

Full employment

This chapter has argued that there cannot be equality of opportunity unless opportunities are there to be grasped. In short, equitable growth depends on the right to a viable livelihood being realised. Unemployment and underemployment are expensive in social and economic terms, as well as being a waste of human potential. Governments therefore have an interest, as well as an obligation, to promote full employment through policies which favour labour-intensive growth and equip workers with the skills necessary to meet changing demands in the labour market. The success of many East Asian countries in creating labour-intensive growth enabled unprecedented numbers of people to escape from poverty in the space of a few decades. This is one regional experience that other developing countries should emulate. Between 1986 and 1993, employment in East Asia grew by over 3% a year, above the rate of labour-force growth, as export-oriented manufacturing expanded rapidly. This figure stands in stark contrast to the rising unemployment and weak or negative export growth of Latin America and sub-Saharan Africa over the same period. East Asia's most successful economies used selective protection and supports for infant industries to promote horizontal diversification (extending the range of unprocessed and semi-processed commodities being produced) and vertical diversification (moving into manufactures with higher added value, such as cars, shipbuilding, and household electrical equipment). The tiger economies employed a diverse range of regulatory mechanisms, some of which failed, and a detailed study of them is beyond the scope of this book. However, what the *dirigiste* interventions of the tigers demonstrate is that close state management of strategic sectors can contribute effectively to pro-poor labour-intensive growth, and so to rapid poverty reduction.

Universal respect for labour rights

Pursuing economic growth at the cost of basic labour rights is inimical to development. On a public-policy level, labour exploitation cannot be tolerated as a source of competitive advantage, and states that are signatories to the UN Universal Declaration of Human Rights are bound to proper observance of Articles 20, 23, and 24:

- Article 20: the right to freedom of association
- Article 23: the right to freedom of employment without discrimination and the right to trade-union membership
- Article 24: the right to rest and leisure and a limitation on working hours.

More specifically, there is a need for an internationally binding social clause enshrining the principles of consultation and dialogue in relations between labour, employees, and government. ILO Conventions 87 and 98 – on freedom of association and the right to organise, and the right to collective bargaining — could form the initial basis of a social clause. Further conventions could be considered for inclusion.

Universal education

Education is the most decisive factor in determining future income-earning opportunities and labour-productivity growth. Employment policies and education policies need to be developed through an integrated and complementary approach. Aside from its implications for poverty eradication, the denial of the most basic educational opportunities for millions of children and adults in the South, often on the basis of gender or ethnicity, represents a violation of human rights on an immense and unacceptable scale. Without equitable access to educational opportunities, the cycle of inequality, poverty, and low growth or no growth which continues to characterise much of the developing world will remain unbroken. Addressing the widening educational inequalities between income groups is a measure that is both urgently needed and affordable. Although it demands a re-ordering of spending priorities and a more efficient use of resources, the challenge facing poor countries to provide a basic primary education for every child is not insurmountable. Ultimately, the fact that tens of millions of children never enter a school is the result of a political choice. The industrialised-country governments have a crucial part to play in extending literacy and other basic skills in developing countries. Aid budgets must be redirected towards meeting basic educational needs; new technologies and new knowledge should be made accessible and affordable for the poorest countries; and agreements on debt relief in return for social investment should be introduced as part of an accelerated and extended debt initiative for the poorest countries.

Sound macro-economic policy

Governments need to display fiscal prudence, especially in the early stages of development, and recognise the pivotal role of private capital as a source of development finance. Without macro-economic stability, labour-intensive growth will fail. Public overspending carries obvious dangers, especially for the poor, who suffer most from devaluations and stabilisation-induced inflation. In Latin America, irresponsible fiscal policies account for much of the region's worsening income inequalities during the last 15 years: in periods of hyperinflation, the poor are least likely to protect the value of their assets, and most likely to suffer from the collapse of local product and labour markets. Fiscal rectitude is not the same thing, however, as 'anti-deficit radicalism': the idea that no budget deficit whatsoever is permissible, regardless of the social costs of rapidly reducing it. In this regard, the IMF's track record in stabilisation and adjustment programmes is not a convincing one, and a more gradual, sequenced approach to stabilisation and restructuring is needed. In particular, unless vulnerable social groups are protected through social provision and programmes supporting alternative livelihoods, trade liberalisation will lead to counter-productive results.

Land redistribution

For the majority of the world's poor, land is a crucial asset. Rural poverty and violent conflict are often the result of inadequate access to land, and the dependency and exploitation that it generates. Land redistribution can be highly effective in reducing rural underemployment and poverty. Implemented effectively, land reform carries fairly small short-term efficiency costs and can provide a springboard for rapid growth in other sectors, given the backward and forward linkages that it creates in the domestic economy. Land redistribution is about extending secure access to land, rather than any particular form of access (such as private ownership based on property contract). The promotion of private individual holdings to the exclusion of alternative forms of access is misplaced. In East Asia, China and Vietnam have both achieved dramatic agricultural productivity growth without privatising land. Land privatisations often run the risk of excluding vulnerable groups, such as indigenous peoples, whose land rights are not codified. Selling off land to the highest bidder results in the poor being excluded from the best land and forced on to the least productive areas. More flexible and equitable approaches to land privatisation should be taken, which recognise that land rights can be rooted in non-commercial principles, and that more secure access can be developed within that framework.

Access to technology

Access to technological inputs, along with land, is a major determinant of poverty and inequality. This is especially the case among rural populations. Access to high-yield varieties of crops, and fertilisers and pesticides, where used as part of a broader rural development strategy, can bring significant benefits to rural households. Inserting developing-country rural producers into liberalised agricultural markets without subsidised access to these inputs is inconsistent under the current system of unfair advantage enjoyed by the industrialised countries, which subsidise their farmers to 40% of the value of their agricultural output, or $180bn, every year.

Credit and savings

Access to credit and savings facilities can help the poor to secure a viable livelihood, providing insurance and opportunities for longer-term investment. Creditor flexibility, responsiveness, and minimal transaction costs are essential. The experience of microfinance schemes in a broad range of developing-country contexts demonstrates that the poor can be efficient and reliable savers and investors, and that sustainable facilities bring wider benefits to society through increases in aggregate demand and lower levels of dependency.

Physical and communications infrastructure

Both rural and urban livelihoods depend on people being able to reach markets and respond to information, from commodity-price signals to formal labour-market opportunities. In cities, this requires an efficient and accessible public transport system, which lowers transaction costs for the poor, who typically live on the periphery of urban areas. In rural areas, the more isolated the area, the higher the transport costs and input prices. Producers suffer from lower prices, and communities are caught in a vicious cycle of poverty, low productivity, and low investment. Feeder roads, stable prices for key commodities, and affordable telecommunications can all help to redress the urban bias and promote more equitable participation in economic growth.

4 Policy recommendations for growth, equity, and poverty reduction

The conclusion of this report reflects the two messages stated in the opening chapter: *poverty is not inevitable*, and *equitable growth is a necessary condition of poverty eradication*. Lessons can be learned, and public-policy recommendations can be made, by examining the recent experiences of societies that have achieved equitable growth. While some societies have successfully developed in the post-war world, and most have made progress in terms of human development, the future challenges remain enormous. For the majority of developing countries, the sort of sustained growth and human development achieved in the most successful East Asian economies remains elusive. For many of the least developed countries, especially in sub-Saharan Africa, economic viability is the immediate challenge.

The causes of poverty and inequality, and the policy responses needed to address them, are complex. Yet it is clear that the global economic and political status quo has failed to address effectively the scale and depth of poverty and inequality. An alternative agenda is urgently needed, one which prioritises the needs of the poor and is committed to equitable and lasting development. As the previous chapters have shown, distributional concerns should be at the heart of poverty-eradication strategies. This is because distribution has a direct impact on the incidence and depth of poverty: inequality slows growth and the rate of poverty reduction, as well as being socially and politically costly.

The foundations for this alternative agenda already exist. Over the past decade a new consensus has emerged about the importance of placing poverty eradication at the heart of macro-economic strategy. Increasingly, the UN agencies and the World Bank have recognised that distributional issues are central to poverty eradication. The United

Nations Social Summit, held in Copenhagen in 1995, reflected this new consensus and gave added impetus to poverty-eradication efforts. More than 180 governments, together with the UN agencies and the World Bank, agreed to work collectively towards the goal of halving the incidence of poverty by 2015.

Yet there remains a gap between declarations and commitments to reduce poverty, and actual policy implementation on the ground. Poverty eradication continues to be subordinated to macro-economic strategy, and treated by many governments as an 'extra', to bolt on to pro-growth strategies. Meanwhile political expediency motivates too many governments to avoid addressing the problem of wealth inequalities, and as a result the effectiveness of policies designed to benefit people living in poverty is diminished. Closing this gap between the rhetoric and reality on poverty eradication requires two changes.

First, the UN and Bretton Woods system needs to become better equipped to take the lead in poverty-eradication efforts. This requires increased funding for the UN agencies, but also requires the UN agencies to use their resources more efficiently. A clearer division of labour between the IMF and the World Bank is also an urgent priority. The IMF has acquired excessive influence over the development agenda in poor countries, while remaining unaccountable, undemocratic, and lacking in the necessary skills to tackle poverty effectively. The IMF should play a diminished but also more focused advisory role in the formulation of macro-economic policy, within the development of national poverty-eradication strategies.

Second, a change is needed in the way in which the role of the state is viewed. The reaction on the part of liberal economists in the 1980s to the failures of states to function effectively, particularly in the low-income countries, led to a largely sterile state-versus-markets debate. More damagingly, it provided a rationale for the chronic underfunding of public services and infrastructure. As Chapter 2 illustrated, one result of the erosion of state capacity in many developing countries was widespread neglect of poor people, who often depend heavily on public services and were unable to meet new costs shifted on to households through public disinvestments. While states cannot mechanistically effect development simply by getting all the right policies into place, an effective and active government and legal system are necessary conditions for its achievement. In short, people develop themselves, but they need the tools to do it. The importance of the state in providing an enabling environment for poverty eradication is undiminished.

Social investment

■ *Equitable access* to health and education services is an essential foundation of rapid growth and efficient poverty reduction. It is also a basic right. Ensuring equitable access to basic social services requires a needs-based approach to demand. States should provide services with a high public-goods content, and develop policies that counter institutional biases and recognise the particular needs of rural populations, the urban poor, and vulnerable social groups.

■ *Spending composition* should prioritise primary facilities both in health and education, where the social returns are highest. Obviously it is essential for the poorest countries to strike a balance between meeting the most basic rights and needs of their citizens and investing in secondary and tertiary education facilities, but decisions on expenditure should be informed by the fact that social returns are lowest and private returns are highest in the secondary and tertiary sectors.

■ *Public spending* is needed to guarantee equitable access to basic rights. Depending on the market mechanism to deliver basic needs tends to be disequalising, and often has disastrous results for vulnerable groups. A shift away from out-of-pocket payments to meeting basic needs — particularly for mothers and children — through the state is a necessary condition of equitable growth.

■ *An end to waste*. Misallocated and misappropriated public money carries especially high opportunity costs for the poor. Progressive revenue-raising policies and public-spending patterns which prioritise the needs of the poor are essential for equitable and sustained economic growth. Overspending on the military, subsidisation of loss-making parastatals, and state corruption are universal problems, but in many developing countries they prevail in extreme forms. Pay and incentive structures which discourage corruption in government and the public sector should be developed. Military expenditure should be minimised, and discretionary spending should under no circumstances exceed combined social-sector spending. Loss-making parastatals should have their subsidies spent more productively on social investment and training programmes for laid-off workers.

■ *International action* is urgently needed to support the poorest countries' efforts to provide basic social services to their populations. This needs to take two forms. First, donor support from industrialised countries to developing countries should be both increased from its current levels and directed towards priority areas in the poorest countries – areas such as health, water, education, and rural infrastructure. Aid should be increased on a country basis from its current average of about 0.3% of rich-country GDP to 0.7% of GDP — the level recommended by the UN. An international timetable for achieving this should be agreed. Aid needs to be better directed to those countries where unmet needs and resource constraints are greatest. In this respect, at least 50% of ODA should be directed to the least developed countries, and at least 20% targeted for basic social services. Secondly, debt relief should be directed to fund poverty-reduction plans, with generous and flexible relief for governments committed to poverty eradication, and able to demonstrate the capacity to make effective use of budget savings from debt reduction. The IMF–World Bank Heavily Indebted Poor Country scheme ('HIPC') needs to be accelerated and extended so that the poorest countries can receive substantial benefits in the short term.

Livelihoods

■ *Viable livelihood opportunities* must be provided, to generate growth to reduce poverty. Underemployment and unemployment cut people off from the benefits of growth, and are socially destructive as well as economically wasteful. Conversely, full employment ensures that the benefits of growth are distributed more widely. Full employment is both a feasible target for individual governments to adopt, and a necessary condition of poverty eradication. Governments have a responsibility to intervene and create incentives and interventions so that people in poverty have viable livelihood opportunities. While labour-intensive growth is both possible and essential to the success of poverty-reduction strategies, it is not a sufficient condition. Growth also needs to be 'pro-poor', with effectively regulated labour markets that prevent exploitation and unfair treatment of workers.

■ *Universal respect for labour rights* is the keystone of pro-poor growth. Governments are already bound to observance of the Universal Declaration of Human Rights, but there is a case for a binding and enforceable social clause to protect the most basic rights of workers, based on ILO Conventions 87 and 98 — the rights to freedom of association and collective bargaining — with a system of sanctions to support it. In a rapidly globalising world, an internationally binding social clause would complement the regulatory framework for trade and investment already developed through the World Trade Organisation.

■ *Universal education* is a prerequisite of any employment strategy designed to raise the capabilities of the poor, and education and training are essential foundations of economic growth. The scale of the education deficit in the poorest countries is one of the greatest obstacles to economic growth and poverty eradication, and requires both increased resources and reform of the education sector for the current crisis to be resolved. Education-sector reform should make education-related and employment-related objectives complementary, with children and adults trained in broadly relevant skills for use in securing a livelihood.

■ *Macro-economic stability* is especially important in the early stages of development, and without it labour-intensive growth will be jeopardised. Public-sector overspending, weakly regulated financial markets, and overvalued exchange rates all have potentially devastating consequences for the poor and for long-term economic growth. Fiscal rectitude is important, but a sequenced and gradual approach to stabilisation and restructuring is also necessary to avoid counter-productive recessionary effects.

■ *Land redistribution* can be highly effective, where it is part of a broad rural development strategy, in reducing rural underemployment. Because asset distribution is the principal determinant of inequality, redistributing land more equitably can foster growth and poverty reduction. Smallholder farming is both labour-intensive and efficient, and can provide a springboard for rapid growth in other sectors. To be effective, land redistribution should be combined with other pro-poor measures, such as access to micro-credit and irrigation programmes.

■ *Access to technology* is crucial to rural development. High-yield varieties of crops and access to fertilisers and pesticides can increase rural productivity and income levels. However, staples such as sorghum, millet, and cassava, consumed by the majority of the poor in Africa, have been neglected by the green revolution. Production in sub-Saharan Africa has stagnated, and food insecurity will be resolved only by innovating in high-yield strains of these crops, developing intermediate technologies, and promoting the use of local knowledge in such areas as intercropping and agroforestry.

■ *Physical and communications infrastructure.* The rural poor in particular live in marginal areas with high transaction costs, which often trap them in poverty. Unpaved roads and a lack of access to public transport often isolate rural producers from external markets, and make them vulnerable to monopolies and monopsonies. Communications infrastructure is often poorly developed in the countryside, making it more difficult for rural producers to respond to market signals. Redressing the bias against rural producers requires developing physical and communications infrastructure in the countryside. Feeder-road programmes, regulation and support of public transport, and the expansion of telecommunications systems can help to promote equitable participation in economic growth.

Globalisation, poverty, and equity

■ *Controls on foreign direct investment* are needed to ensure that labour rights and environmental standards are maintained and that developing countries gain from Foreign Direct Investment. Because FDI often takes the form of large projects with potentially damaging social and environmental effects, commissioning independent bodies to assess the social and environmental impact of controversial projects can act as an important check. The Multilateral Agreement on Investment, formulated by the OECD, would prohibit restrictions on majority foreign ownership, and employment conditions. These were common policies in the first generation of tiger economies, where FDI was successfully harnessed, creating employment with high added value. Without the capacity to apply conditions to foreign investors, governments have limited scope to promote technology transfers and linkages with domestic producers, and to develop a competitive advantage.

■ *Reform of the World Trade Organisation.* Without reform of international trade and investment regimes, equitable growth and poverty reduction will be undermined. The Uruguay Round was a genuine opportunity to introduce international trade rules which balanced the needs and interests of the industrialised and the developing countries.

Apart from some progress on tariff reduction, this opportunity was largely wasted. Whereas tariffs for the industrialised countries will have been brought down substantially to below 4%, average levels remain high for a number of developing countries, especially in West Africa and South Asia. Commodities such as leather, oilseeds, textile fibres, and beverages will see tariffs continue to rise on the final-stage product, restricting the foreign-exchange earnings of some of the poorest countries. In the area of agricultural liberalisation, the WTO rules carry similarly damaging implications for the poor. Tariff escalation should be ended, deeper tariff cuts are needed, and rules of origin should be clarified. Reforms are also needed to broaden the membership of the WTO and increase the participation of poor countries. The complex rules and procedures of the WTO require member states to commit financial and technical resources that the poorest countries typically lack. As a result, their interests are not being fairly represented through the WTO. A fund set up by the wealthiest WTO members to help to provide low-income countries with the resources needed to join and participate effectively in the WTO could help to address this democratic deficit.

■ *Regulation of financial markets* is an urgent priority, on both the national and international levels. No other area of global trade is currently so under-regulated. Effective regulation of banks, with measures to deter risky lending and encourage efficient investment, needs to be combined with a more gradualist and cautious approach to financial market liberalisation than that currently promoted by the International Monetary Fund. On the international level, a foreign-exchange transaction tax could slow down capital movements and give governments more time to respond to and avoid the more serious knock-on effects of currency crises. Second, a formal regulatory body to oversee financial markets, equipped with the powers to demand full disclosure from financial institutions and restrict speculative activity, is needed.

■ *Commodity-market reform and diversification.* Despite recent failed attempts at supply management in primary-commodity production, supply control remains a short-term imperative if market volatility is to be avoided. In the longer term, commodity dependency can be resolved only by diversifying the export base of primary-commodity exporters. The revenue from an international transaction tax on foreign-exchange markets could finance an internationally administered support fund, to be used to promote investments in commodity processing and horizontal diversification. Meanwhile, industrialised-country fixed-term trade preferences need to be extended and broadened, providing an adjustment period for countries heavily dependent on primary commodities.

Notes

Chapter 1

1 Aristotle, *The Nicomachean Ethics* I (5), translation by Ross, Oxford: Oxford University Press 1980.
2 A. Smith, *The Wealth of Nations*, Harmondsworth: Penguin 1986.
3 A. Sen, *Commodities and Capabilities*, Amsterdam: North Holland 1985; A. Sen, 'Agency and well-being: the development agenda', in H. Noeleen, and S. Kapoor, *A Commitment to the World's Women — Perspectives for Development for Beijing and Beyond*, New York: UNIFEM 1995.
4 ECLAC, *Social Panorama of Latin America 1995*, Washington DC: ECLAC 1995.
5 The case of the Enhanced Structural Adjustment Facility (ESAF) undertaken in Zambia during the early 1990s is instructive in this regard. See *IMF External Evaluation of the ESAF: Report by a Group of Independent Experts*, Washington D.C: IMF 1998.
6 UNDP: *Human Development Report 1996*; World Bank: *World Development Report 1995*.
7 J. Drèze, *Widows in Rural India*, London: STICERD (26) 1990.
8 N. Kabeer, *Reversed Realities: Gender Hierarchies in Development Thought*, London: Verso 1994.
9 J. Drèze and A. Sen, *Hunger and Public Action*, Oxford: Oxford University Press 1989.
10 *The Economist*, 'A survey of Cuba: heroic illusions', 6 April1999; 'Survey: The Americas shift towards private health care ', 8 May 1999.
11 K. S. Kim, 'Income distribution and poverty: an interregional comparison', *World Development* 25 (11) 1997.
12 See for example D. Lal and H. Myint, *The Political Economy of Poverty, Equity and Growth*, Oxford: Oxford University Press 1996.
13 K. Griffin, *Alternative Strategies for Economic Development*, London: Macmillan 1989.

14 R. Berry and W. Cline, *Agrarian Structure and Productivity in Developing Countries,* Geneva: ILO 1979; K. Deininger and K. Binswanger, *The Evolution of the World Bank's Land Policy,* Washington DC: World Bank 1998.

15 UNDP, *Human Development in South Asia,* Karachi: Oxford University Press 1997; UNICEF, *State of the World's Children 1997,* New York: UNICEF 1997; World Bank, *World Development Indicators 1997,* Washington DC: World Bank 1997.

16 Calculated from World Bank *World Development Indicators 1998* (Washington DC: World Bank 1998).

17 See J. Stiglitz, 'Whither Reform?', paper delivered to World Bank Conference on Development Economics, Washington DC, 30 April 1999.

18 *Financial Times,* 'Corruption in the spotlight', 16 September 1997; UNDP *Human Development Report* 1991 and 1997.

19 World Bank, *Everyone's Miracle? Revisiting Poverty and Inequality in East Asia,* Washington DC: World Bank 1997; *Far Eastern Economic Review,* 'Under the volcano', 13 March 1997.

20 World Bank, 'Crime and violence as obstacles to growth in Latin America', *World Bank News,* 6 March 1997.

21 T. McKinley and D. Alarcon, 'The prevalence of rural poverty in Mexico', *World Development* Vol. 23 (9) 1995.

22 D. Corry and A. Glyn, 'The macroeconomics of equality, stability and growth' in D. Miliband and A. Glyn, *Paying for Inequality: The Economic Costs of Social Injustice,* London: IPPR / Rivers Oram Press 1994; UNDP *Human Development Report 1996.*

23 K. Deininger and L. Squire, *Does Inequality Matter? Re-examining the links between growth and inequality,* Washington DC: World Bank 1996.

24 OECD, *Employment Outlook,* Paris: OECD 1997.

25 World Bank, *Everyone's Miracle? Revisiting Poverty and Inequality in East Asia,* Washington DC: World Bank 1997.

26 P. Levine, *Is Asian Growth a Threat to the West?,* University of Surrey, Department of Economics Working Paper 97:1.

27 K. Griffin, *Alternative Strategies for Economic Development,* 1989.

28 K. Watkins, *Economic Growth with Equity: Lessons from East Asia,* Oxford: Oxfam 1998.

29 ECLAC, *The Equity Gap,* Santiago, April 1997.

30 V. Bulmer-Thomas, *The Economic Model in Latin America and its Impact on Income Distribution and Poverty,* London: Macmillan 1996.

31 K. Watkins, op. cit.

32 World Bank, *India: Achievements and Challenges in Reducing Poverty* report 16483-IN, May 1997. This figure is reached using the extremely low Indian government poverty line of Rs49 per capita per month at October 73–June 74 rural prices. Using the Bank poverty line gives a poverty figure of 52.5% (1981-1995 average).

33 W.A. Lewis, *The Theory of Economic Growth*, London: Allen and Unwin 1955.

34 N. Birdsall, and F. Jaspersen (eds.), *Pathways to Growth: Comparing East Asia and Latin America*, Washington DC: IDB 1997; ILO, *Poverty and Landlessness in Rural Asia* Geneva: ILO 1977.

35 H. Chenery, *Redistribution with Growth: Policies to improve income distribution in developing countries in the context of economic growth*, World Bank / IDS joint study, London: Oxford University Press 1974.

36 A. Alesina and D. Rodrik, 'Distributive politics and economic growth', *Quarterly Journal of Economics* CIX (2) 1994.

37 N. Stern and J. Stiglitz, *A Framework for a Development Strategy in a Market Economy: objectives, scope, institutions and instruments*, London: EBRD Working Paper 20 1997.

38 A. Sen, *What's the Point of a Development Strategy?*, London: STICERD 1997.

39 Hong Kong is the exception in not having pursued dirigiste policies. Singapore, Taiwan, and South Korea all maintained tight market controls and made frequent use of interventionist policy.

40 A. Amsden, *Asia's Next Giant: South Korea and Late Industrialisation*, Oxford: Oxford University Press 1989; R. Wade, *Governing the Market: Economic Theory and the Role of Government in East Asian Industrialisation*, Princeton: Princeton University Press 1990.

Chapter 2

1 For a summary of the arguments, see for example G. Psacaropoulos, 'Returns to investments in education: a global update', *World Development* 22 (9) 1994.

2 C. Colclough, 'Who should learn to pay? An assessment of neo-liberal approaches to education policy' in C. Colclough and J. Manor (eds.), *States or Markets: Neo-liberalism and the Development Policy Debate*, Oxford: Clarendon Press 1991.

3 Oxfam believes that every person has a basic right to a home, clean water, enough to eat, a safe environment, protection from violence, equality of opportunity, a say in their future, education, a livelihood,

and health care. See *Words into Action: Basic Rights and the Campaign against World Poverty*, Oxford: Oxfam 1995.

4 Adam Smith, *Theory of Moral Sentiments* Vol. IV, Oxford: Oxford University Press 1976.

5 *Financial Times,* 'Malaysia skills shortage hits home', 20 August 1997; *Far Eastern Economic Review,* 'Managing, barely', 28 August 1997.

6 World Bank, *Confronting AIDS: Public Priorities in a Global Epidemic,* New York: Oxford University Press 1997.

7 J. Drèze and A. Sen, *Indian Development: Selected Regional Perspectives,* Delhi: Oxford University Press 1996.

8 T. McKinley and D. Alarcón, 'Rural poverty in Mexico', *World Development* Vol.23 (9) 1995; ECLAC, *Social Panorama of Latin America 1994,* Washington DC: ECLAC 1994.

9 World Bank, *Everyone's Miracle? Revisiting Poverty and Inequality in East Asia,* Washington DC: World Bank 1997.

10 T. Nahar, 'The Bangladesh Garment Industry, Time for Reform', Oxford: Oxfam 1996.

11 Literacy in China is recorded as basic competence in any local language, including Tibetan. The figures do not therefore reflect the low numbers of Chinese-speakers in Tibet.

12 S. J. Jejeebhoy, *Women's Education, Autonomy, and Reproductive Behaviour: Experience from Developing Countries,* Oxford: Oxford University Press 1995.

13 J. Drèze and A. Sen 1996, op. cit.; T. N. Krishnan, 'The route to social development in Kerala: social intermediation and public action' in S. Mehrotra and R. Jolly, *Development with a Human Face: Experiences in Social Achievement and Economic Growth,* Oxford: Clarendon Press 1997; R. Jeffrey, *Politics, Women and Well-Being: How Kerala Became a Model,* Oxford: Oxford University Press 1992.

14 K. Griffin, *Alternative Strategies for Economic Development,* London: Macmillan 1989.

15 N. Birdsall, D. Ross, and R. Sabot, 'Education, growth and inequality' in N. Birdsall and F. Jaspersen, *Pathways to Growth: Comparing East Asia and Latin America,* Washington DC: IDB 1997.

16 S. Morley and A. Silva, *Problems and Performance in Primary Education: Why do Systems Differ?* Washington DC: IDB 1994.

17 Inter-American Development Bank, *Economic and Social Progress in Latin America 1996: Making Social Services Work,* Washington DC: IDB 1996.

18 World Bank, *World Development Report 1995: Workers in an Integrating World,* Washington DC: World Bank.

19 D. Black, C. Smith, J. Morris, and P. Townsend, *Inequalities in Health: report of a research working group*, London: Department of Health and Social Security 1980.

20 This following section draws extensively on C. Colclough, *Marketizing Education and Health in Developing Countries: Miracle or Mirage?* Oxford: Oxford University Press 1997.

21 G. Psacharopoulos, *World Bank Research News* 4 (1), Washington DC: World Bank 1983, and *World Development* 22 (9) 1994. For discussion of rates of return to education — in sub-Saharan Africa particularly — see Appleton, Bennell et al., *Journal of International Development* Vol.8 (3) 1996 .

22 *The Economist*, 'Mishap in the operating theatre', 2 August 1997.

23 *British Dental Association News*, Vol.7 (6) 1994.

24 A. Hirschman, *Exit, Voice and Loyalty*, London: Harvard University Press 1970.

25 E. Ostrom, *Governing the Commons: The Evolution of Institutions for Collective Action*, New York: Cambridge University Press 1990.

26 B. Yang, 'Issues in health care delivery: the case of Korea' in D. W. Dunlop and J. M. Martins, *An International Assessment of Health Care Financing: Lessons for Developing Countries*, Washington DC: World Bank 1995.

27 U. E. Reinhardt, 'The health system of the United States: lessons for other countries' in Dunlop and Martins, *World Development Indicators 1997*, Washington DC: World Bank.

28 L. Aiguo, *Welfare Changes in China during the Economic Reforms*, Helsinki: WIDER 1996; IDS, 'Health in transition: reforming rural China's health services', *IDS Bulletin* Volume 28 (1) 1997; D. Yu, 'Decentralisation of Finance System, Price Reform and Commune System Disintegration: The Changes in China's Health Care System' (draft), WIDER project meeting paper 1997.

29 J. Drèze and A. Sen, *Hunger and Public Action*, Oxford: Oxford University Press 1989.

30 A. Creese and J. Kutzin, 'Lessons from cost recovery in health', in C. Colclough 1997, op. cit..

31 K. Watkins, 'Cost Recovery and Equity in the Health Sector: issues for developing countries', draft paper prepared for WIDER, February 1997.

32 Ibid.

33 C. Colclough, 'Education and the market: which parts of the neoliberal solution are correct?' *World Development* Vol.24 (4) 1996.

34 UNICEF, *State of the World's Children 1999*, New York: UNICEF 1999.

35 The Jomtien Conference in March 1990, involving governments, international organisations, and NGOs, adopted the World Declaration on Education for All, as well as country-specific targets for meeting educational needs. See A. Little, W. Hoppers, and R. Gardner, *Beyond Jomtien: Implementing Primary Education for All*, London: Macmillan 1994.

36 UN Economic Commission for Africa, *Economic and Social Survey of Africa 1994-95*, Addis Ababa: UNECA 1995.

37 C. Colclough with K. Lewin, *Educating All the Children: Strategies for Primary Schooling in the South*, Oxford: Oxford University Press 1993.

38 UNESCO, *Statistical Yearbook 1998*, Paris: UNESCO 1998; *World Education Report 1998*, Paris: UNESCO 1998.

39 African Development Bank, *African Development Report 1997*, Oxford: ADB/Oxford University Press.

40 Of the 30 countries with the lowest gross enrolment ratios over the period 1990–1994, 21 were Heavily Indebted Poor Countries (HIPCs), eligible for some debt relief under the new IMF/World Bank initiative, 12 countries were paying out more than 20% of the value of their exports of goods and services in debt-service repayments, while over the period 1985–1994 only four countries had experienced per capita GNP growth rates exceeding 2% (UNDP, UNICEF and World Bank 1997).

41 Inter-American Development Bank, *Economic and Social Progress in Latin America 1996: Making Social Services Work*.

42 This section follows closely Tendler and Freedheim, 'Trust in a rent-seeking world: health and government transformed in northeast Brazil', *World Development* Vol.22 (12) 1994.

43 IDB, *Economic and Social Progress in Latin America 1996: Making Social Services Work*.

44 ECLAC, *Social Panorama of Latin America 1994*.

45 J. Drèze and A. Sen 1996, op. cit.

46 UNICEF, *State of the World's Children 1997*, New York: UNICEF 1997.

47 *The Guardian*, 'Blunder blocks Peru's generals from playing with new toys', 5 June 1997.

48 UNDP, *Human Development Report 1997*, New York: UNDP 1997; Campaign Against the Arms Trade, *The Supply of UK Military Equipment to Nigeria*, London: CAAT, March 1996.

49 UNDP, *Human Development in South Asia 1997*, Karachi: UNDP 1997; UNICEF, *State of the World's Children 1997*, New York: UNICEF 1997; World Bank, *World Development Indicators 1997*, Washington DC: World Bank 1997.

50 Colclough with Lewin, op. cit.
51 Economist Intelligence Unit, *Uganda Country Profile 1996-97,* London: EIU 1997.
52 Duncan Green, *Silent Revolution: The Rise of Market Economics in Latin America,* London: Cassell/LAB 1995.
53 World Bank, *Assessing Aid: what works, what doesn't, and why,* New York: Oxford University Press 1998.
54 Development Assistance Committee, *DAC Chairman's Report 1998,* Paris: OECD 1998.
55 For a detailed discussion of education performance indicators, see Colclough with Lewin, op. cit.
56 G. Kingdon, *Private Schooling in India: Size, Nature and Equity Effects,* London: STICERD 1996.
57 N. Prescott, *Poverty, Social Services and Safety Nets in Vietnam,* Washington DC: World Bank 1997.
58 Colclough with Lewin, op. cit.
59 J.Miller Del Rosso and T. Marek, *Class Action: Improving School Performance in the Developing World through Better Health and Nutrition,* Washington DC: World Bank 1996.
60 World Food Programme, *Thematic Evaluation: West African School Canteen Projects,* Rome: WFP 1995.
61 H. Bergmann, 'Quality of education and the demand for education — evidence from developing countries', *International Review of Education* Vol.42 (6) 1996.
62 UN Economic Commission for Africa, *Economic and Social Survey of Africa 1994-95.*
63 *The Economist,* 'Moi, lord of Kenya's empty dance', 15 May 1999.

Chapter 3

1 The informal sector can be defined as the small-scale, insecure, household-based, and usually untaxed selling of goods and services. It accounts for the majority of livelihoods in the urban South. For a discussion of the informal sector, see for example V. E. Tokman, *Beyond Regulation: The Informal Economy in Latin America,* Boulder and London: Lynne Rienner/ILO 1992.
2 R. Chambers, *Poverty and Livelihoods: Whose Reality Counts?* UNDP Roundtable on Global Change, Stockholm, July 1994.
3 S.M. Dev, 'Experience of India's employment guarantee scheme: lessons for development policy', *Development Policy Review* Vol. 14

(3) 1996; J. Drèze and A. Sen, *Hunger and Public Action*, Oxford: Oxford University Press 1989.

4   See M. Qizilbash, 'Pluralism and well-being indices', *World Development* Vol. 25 (12) 1997.

5   The figure is from the International Office on Migration (IOM) in Geneva.

6   Economist Intelligence Unit, *Bolivia Country Profile 1995-96*, London: EIU 1996; Washington Office on Latin America, *Fueling Failure: US International Drug Control Policy*, Washington D.C: WOLA 1995.

7   UNDP, *Human Development Report 1996*, New York: UNDP 1996.

8   D. Miliband and A. Glyn, *Paying for Inequality: The Economic Costs of Social Injustice*, London: IPPR / Rivers Oram Press 1994.

9   OECD, *Employment Outlook*, Paris: OECD 1997.

10 ECLAC, *Social Panorama of Latin America 1995*, New York: ECLAC 1995. The ECLAC poverty line is based in part on the cost of a local food basket, and can yield widely divergent poverty figures from those obtained by using the World Bank line.

11 See P. Drucker, *Post-Capitalist Society*, London: Butterworth-Heinemann 1993; L. Thurow, *The Future of Capitalism: How Today's Economic Forces Shape Tomorrow's World*, London: Nicholas Brealey 1996.

12 UNDP, *Human Development Report 1998*, Oxford: Oxford University Press 1998.

13 Until recently the World Bank used an income-poverty line of $2 a day in Latin America. This was partly intended to reflect the fact that over three-quarters of Latin Americans live in urban areas, where living costs are higher. Yet this fails to capture the capability constraints faced by city-dwellers. See IDS, 'Urban poverty: a new research agenda', *IDS Bulletin* Volume 28 (2) 1997.

14 Interview with Oxfam field staff, Brazil, April 1998.

15 B. Anderson, *Labour Exchange: Patterns of Migration in Asia*, London: CIIR 1997; Panos, *The Hidden Costs of AIDS: The Challenge of HIV to Development*, London: Panos 1992.

16 World Business, *So Near to Meltdown*, Spring 1995.

17 C. Heredia and M. Purcell, *The Wrong Path: The World Bank's Country Assistance Strategy for Mexico*, Mexico City: Equipo Pueblo 1996.

18 *Financial Times*, 'Hazardous trades bring pollution and health fears down Mexico way', 10 June 1997.

19 *Guardian*, 'Profits of doom on the border of blight', 21 August 1992.

20 *Financial Times*, 'Border companies criticised', 30 December 1998.

21 H. Browne, *For Richer, For Poorer: Shaping US–Mexican Integration*, London: Latin America Bureau 1994.

22 See H. de Soto, *The Other Path: the invisible revolution in the third world*, London: Tauris 1989.

23 Alan Gilbert, *The Latin American City*, London: Latin America Bureau 1994.

24 I. Grunberg, 'Double jeopardy: globalisation, liberalization and the fiscal squeeze', *World Development* Vol. 26 (4) 1998.

25 ILO, *Child Labour: Targeting the Intolerable*, Geneva: ILO 1996.

26 J. Drèze, *Widows in Rural India*, London: STICERD (26) 1990.

27 B. Anderson, op. cit.

28 The term was coined in M. Lipton, *Why Poor People Stay Poor: Urban Bias in World Development*, London: Temple Smith 1977; his argument is drawn on here.

29 K. Deininger and K. Binswanger, *The Evolution of the World Bank's Land Policy*, Washington DC: World Bank 1998.

30 Economist Intelligence Unit, *Zimbabwe Country Profile 1996-97*, London: EIU 1997; K. Watkins, *The Oxfam Poverty Report*, Oxford: Oxfam 1995.

31 K. Griffin, *Alternative Strategies for Economic Development*, London: St. Martin's Press 1989.

32 R. Wade, *Governing the Market: Economic Theory and the Role of Government in East Asian Industrialisation*, Princeton: Princeton University Press 1990; H-J. Chang, *The Political Economy of Industrial Policy*, London: St. Martin's Press 1994.

33 N. Kabeer and P.K. Murthy, *Compensating for Institutional Exclusion? Lessons from Indian Government and Non-Government Credit Interventions for the Poor*, IDS Discussion Paper 356, 1996.

34 S. Johnson and B. Rogaly, *Microfinance and Poverty Reduction*, Oxford: Oxfam 1997.

35 P. Strachan and C. Peters, *Empowering Communities: A Casebook from West Sudan*, Oxford: Oxfam 1997.

36 A. Goetz and R. Sen Gupta, 'Who takes the credit? Gender, power and control over loan use in rural credit programmes in Bangladesh', *World Development* 24 (1) 1996.

37 H. Hill, *The Indonesian Economy since 1966*, Cambridge: Cambridge University Press 1996.

38 M. Lipton, 'Market relaxation and agricultural development' in J. Manor and C. Colclough, *States or Markets: Neoliberalism and the Development Policy Debate*, Oxford: Clarendon Press 1991.

39 K. Griffin and T. McKinley, *Implementing a Human Development Strategy*, London: Macmillan 1994.

40 World Bank, *The East Asian Miracle: Economic Growth and Public Policy*, New York: Oxford University Press 1993.

41 At the end of the Uruguay Round tariff reductions in 2001, the average tariff on manufactured exports will be only 3%, in contrast to 47% at the end of World War II (UNDP Human Development Report 1997).

42 UNCTAD, *World Investment Report 1997*, New York: UNCTAD 1997.

43 A. Balasubranamyam and V.N. Balasubranamyam, 'Singer, services and software', *World Development* Vol.25 (11) 1997.

44 J. Carillo, 'Flexible production in the auto sector: industrial reorganisation at Ford-Mexico', *World Development* Vol.23 (1) 1995.

45 Calculated from M. Davenport and S. Page, *World Trade Reform: Do Developing Countries Gain or Lose?* London: ODI Special Report 1994.

46 UNCTAD, *Trade and Development Report 1997*, New York: UNCTAD 1997.

47 Excluding India and China. World Bank, *World Development Report 1997: The State in a Changing World*, Washington DC: World Bank 1997.

48 ILO, *World Employment 1995*, Geneva: ILO 1995.

49 H. Singer, 'The distribution of gains between investing and borrowing countries', *American Economic Review* Vol.11, May 1950.

50 A. Wood, 'Does Trade Reduce Wage Inequality in Developing Countries?', paper delivered at Queen Elizabeth House 40th anniversary conference, Oxford.

51 Ibid.

52 UNCTAD, *Trade and Development Report 1997*. The ratio of the seven poorest to seven richest countries is calculated at purchasing-power parity.

53 Ibid.

54 *Financial Times*, 'Unemployment in Brazil set to grow', 9 October 1997.

55 S. Halebsky and J. Harris, *Capital, Power and Inequality in Latin America*, Boulder: Westview 1995.

56 T. Killick, *Explaining Africa's Post-Independence Development Experiences*, London: ODI Working Paper 60 1992; A. Maizels, 'Commodities in crisis: an overview of the main issues', *World Development* 15 (5) 1987.

57 A. Maizels, R. Bacon, and G. Mavrotas, *Commodity Supply Management by Producing Countries*, Oxford: Oxford University Press 1997.

58 ILO, *The ILO, Standard Setting, and Globalisation: Report of the Director General*, Geneva: ILO 1997; C. Le Quesne, *Reforming World Trade: The Social and Environmental Priorities*, Oxford: Oxfam 1996.

59 Oxfam supports the ILO's campaign for governments to individually ratify and implement core conventions, and is pressing for voluntary codes of conduct to be adopted by firms. See R. Mayne, *The International Dimensions of Work: Some Implications for the UK*, a paper for the Work and Opportunities Programme of the Joseph Rowntree Foundation, Oxford: Oxfam 1997.

Index